I HEART MOM

Stories of women held together by the strongest of threads in the thin frayed edges of motherhood.

www.relevantpagespress.com
relevantpagespress@gmail.com

Scripture quotations are taken from the following biblical translations: Scripture quotations marked (TLB) are taken from The Living Bible copyright © 1971. Used by permission of Tyndale House Publishers, Inc., Carol Stream, Illinois 60188. All rights reserved.

Scripture quotations are taken from the Holy Bible, New Living Translation, copyright ©1996, 2004, 2007, 2013, 2015 by Tyndale House Foundation. Used by permission of Tyndale House Publishers, Inc., Carol Stream, Illinois 60188. All rights reserved.

Scripture quotations from THE MESSAGE. Copyright © by Eugene H. Peterson 1993, 1994, 1995, 1996, 2000, 2001, 2002. Used by permission of NavPress. All rights reserved. Represented by Tyndale House Publishers, Inc.

Scripture taken from the New King James Version®. Copyright © 1982 by Thomas Nelson. Used by permission. All rights reserved.

Cover design by Golden Lion Design via 99designs.com
Printed in the United States of America.

Book Layout © 2017 BookDesignTemplates.com
Edited by Dana Frazeur.

I Heart Mom. -- 1st ed.
ISBN 978-0-9982211-8-2

For mothers everywhere

"You never know how strong you are until being strong is the only choice you have."

—BOB MARLEY

CONTENTS

Foreword

By Jennifer Tubbiolo

The women who penned the essays found inside this anthology are every bit as extraordinary as the stories themselves. Each has come from a place of her own individual trials and struggles, yet there are common themes running through each essay to which every mother can relate. Themes of pain and loss, of expectations unmet, and of inconceivable joy and exhilaration. They are themes I recognize in my own story of motherhood, and in my mother's, and in her mother's before her. Motherhood doesn't change with the times and it isn't influenced by culture or trends. The love a mother has for her child, whether conceived from her own body or not, is one of the bedrocks on which human existence is built. We can count on it.

I look at my fourteen-year-old daughter now and I'm reminded of myself at her age. It was just yesterday she was dressing in plastic princess shoes and swimming with floaties. Today, she knows everything because she saw it on YouTube. If you were to ask her, she would tell you she is absolutely ready to be an adult. How hard could it be, right? Now I understand what my mom must have thought looking at me at fourteen: *If only I can ensure when she steps out into the world on her own it will be as perfect as she envisions it's going to be.* But the truth is, we can't ensure it. Just like our mothers couldn't before us.

The best we can do is give them a foundation of faith, wisdom, and truth. We can be the one in their corner, the one with the advice we've gathered from the rubble of our own mistakes. (But only when advice is asked for, of course. Unsolicited advice can be perceived as judgement when it comes from mothers to adult children.)

But the most important thing we can do for our kids is to continue living our lives well. Even adult children watch their mothers. By continuing to confidently move forward on the path of life, navigating its pitfalls, bumpy terrain, and boulders as they come, we are giving our children a path to follow. I'm grateful for a mother who I can continue to confidently follow as she navigates her own life's path. My prayer is that I, too, will be that beacon of light on the road ahead as my children stumble on their own troubles or stray off into the weeds of life. We can all do that for our kids. We are mothers.

Harriet Turk

FOR THE LOVE OF TIES

I didn't think about it until it was too late.

Andrew had to wear a tie to school.

It's customary for the football players to dress up on game days. I knew this, but I had never equated "dressing up" with wearing a tie—a tie Andrew didn't know how to tie—until now.

Our lifestyle rarely requires Andrew to wear a tie, and in the past when one was required, he's chosen a pre-tied bow tie. But now that he was in high school, he wanted to wear a regular tie.

It was 6:00 a.m., I am a single mom, his dad doesn't live with us, and neither Andrew nor I knew how to tie a tie. In 15 short minutes, we needed to leave for school.

Andrew came barreling down the stairs, freaking out. "Mom, HELP ME. Watch this video and do it." I grabbed his phone, quickly watched a YouTube video, and gave it my best shot. I'm left-handed, and none of the YouTube guru's instructions were translating well as I struggled to understand what to do. Andrew started yelling at me. I understood his frustration. It wasn't my fault, but in his mind at that moment, it was. As his mom, I was supposed to solve this problem *right then*. But I couldn't.

No answer I gave was good enough. I suggested that when we picked up Landon, we could ask Landon's dad for help. "No," said Andrew. I told him it was the only thing I knew to do. We simply weren't able to do this on our own.

He answered more emphatically, "I said, NO."

"Okay then," I replied. "Get in the car. Maybe you can figure it out on the way." Of course, as I drove, our anxiety was off the charts. Both of us handle stressful situations poorly. In fact, we both freak out, and God bless anyone who is in our way.

Every time I made a suggestion, Andrew got a little more upset. The tipping point came when I said, "We will be close to Coach Roedel's house. Let's stop by and let him help you?"

Andrew exploded, "HAVE YOU LOST YOUR MIND? WE CANNOT GO TO COACH'S HOUSE! JUST DRIVE!"

I didn't know what to do. I could feel my son's anxiety, and all I wanted was to make that tie magically tie itself into a perfect, beautiful knot.

When Landon got in the car, he tried to help. But he couldn't do it either. His dad had helped him before he left the house. This fact, alone, transported me into an angry, imaginary conversation with Andrew's dad. This was HIS fault. If our marriage hadn't crumbled, then he would have been there to help our son, and we wouldn't be having this horrible morning. Why couldn't he have taught our son how to tie a freaking tie? Didn't he know Andrew would need to know how to do this? Isn't this a skill all dads teach their sons? Why was I left with this responsibility? It felt like yet another task I was faced with, when it seemed like something he, as the dad, should have done.

I was jolted back to the present as Andrew yelled, "I'm going to get in trouble and every coach is going to start yelling because I don't have on a tie!"

"Andrew, I know coaches understand these things," I reasoned. "I'm sure they have helped many guys with their ties. Please, just go into the locker room and ask one of them for help. They won't care. I swear. They will help you!"

I had barely gotten the words out of my mouth and pulled up to the drop-off area when Andrew completely came unglued. "You don't know these coaches. They expect us to know what to do. I'll be in trouble, and I'll have to deal with it. Thanks, mom. Just thanks." He got out of the car, slammed the door, and stormed away.

It was not the time to call him back to talk about his disrespect, his anger, and his yelling at me when nothing was my fault. Instead, my heart was breaking. What a terrible way to start his day. What an embarrassing time for him. It was his first Friday to dress up with the varsity football team. All he wanted was to fit in and have his tie look right. This was one of those mom moments when I had to drive away and hope it all would work out. As much as I wanted to walk in the locker room and solve this problem for him, I had to drive away and anticipate the next "mom of a teenage boy" moment that would surely materialize when I least expected it.

What were the missing pieces that might be coming up in my son's life that he needed to know—from his dad and/or from me? We don't have a "normal" two-parent home, and in reality, it wasn't his dad's fault he wasn't there on that particular morning. Maybe it was mine. Maybe it was Andrew's. He was 14 years old. He definitely knew before 6:00 a.m. on that Friday morning that he needed to wear a tie, so he should have found out how to tie one. Or maybe it was nobody's fault. Maybe we all needed to be better prepared.

When Andrew walked in the door that night, I asked about the game but what I really wanted to know was what happened when he walked into school that morning. How did he handle the whole tie fiasco? He smiled his shy smile and said that, as he was standing in the locker room watching a YouTube video on his phone, one of his teammates, Kip, walked over and said, "Turk, do you not know how to tie a tie?" When Andrew said he didn't, Kip immediately offered to help. In my son's eyes, that simple act spoke volumes about the kind of guy Kip is. He could have laughed, or he could have made a big deal about Andrew's lack of expertise, but he didn't. He just calmly and quietly came over to help a friend and teammate. To Kip, it was no big deal; he just tied Andrew's tie. But, for this mom, he saved my son's morning and calmed his anxiety.

It's now my personal mission when I conduct leadership retreats and workshops to include a tie-tying activity in my programs. It's for the boys, yes. It's also for the girls so they can help their brothers, boyfriends, or other guy friends.

But mainly, it's for the moms. It's so they don't ever have to experience one of those freak out mornings like I did—at least not about a tie.

Aubrey Atkinson

TWIRLING THROUGH THE UNEXPECTED

As a little girl, I dreamed of being a "mommy" one day. I would carry around my twin Cabbage Patch Kids with me everywhere. I loved them as if they were actual living and breathing babies. I had a stroller, a playpen, and all the "things" needed to take care of them. I would pack a diaper bag and have my mom drag all their stuff with us wherever we went. That is unless I had a sitter lined up (a.k.a. another stuffed animal). The motherhood "gene," fully infiltrated my body from the start. There was never a question in my mind IF I wanted to have a family, only a matter of WHEN it would happen. And, of course, that WHEN would be in my own timing and it was as simple as that. Oh, naivete. What a sweet and innocent thought process it creates.

In September of 2011, a few weeks before my 31st birthday, I married the man of my prayers and dreams. Since I was a tad older than I'd imagined I would be when I got married and I wasn't going to be traveling backward on the age-train anytime soon, we decided to hit the ground running and start a family immediately after we said "I do." Little did we know that our run would quickly turn into a crawl, and then into what felt like we'd completely stalled because we could no longer feel our legs underneath us. We had no idea how difficult and painful, frustrating and heartbreaking, and completely gut-wrenching the simple notion of "starting a family" could be.

By the time the following summer had rolled around, I had probably taken 87 pregnancy tests. Ok, that might be a slight exaggeration, but it sure felt like it. With each new box of "pee sticks" we opened, the thoughts started to creep in that something could be "off" with my body. After one negative test too many, I decided it was time to call my OB/GYN. She asked me to come in and get some blood work done, assuring me it was probably nothing major. She said we would take things one step at a time. Referring me to an infertility specialist would be the very last step she would take.

After I had been given a hypothyroidism diagnosis, we thought we were in the clear. That is until she called me to come in and "chat." Hidden under my file sitting on her desk, I spotted local fertility specialist brochures. At that moment, my world turned upside down. I saw her mouth moving, but couldn't comprehend a single word. I just stared at the brochures, unable to function. When I got into my car, I screamed, letting the brochures fall through my fingers onto my lap. Tears streamed down my face, and my body trembled from shock and fear, from disbelief and pain, and from intense anger. All I could think was: "This has to be a nightmare. Someone PLEASE wake me up!"

I'm not sure how I made it home. I cried more tears than I knew possible. I longed for a body that just "worked." I screamed at God. I cussed Him out! I kicked and punched floors, questioning and begging for this to be taken away. I felt hopeless, yet I knew He was the source of our hope and our strength to walk through this. After many hours and days of feeling utterly broken as individuals and as a couple (our bodies were just supposed to be able to create babies), we decided it was time to make a plan.

For months, innocent questions from well-meaning friends and family had left us shattered. "When are you going to start having kids?" and "Why aren't you pregnant yet?" and "You know you're not getting any younger, right? Time to start popping those babies out!" We were devastated at both our inability to answer those questions positively and with the news we had received of our inability to conceive naturally. Instead of unfairly holding this information hostage, we decided to write an email to our families and close friends answering all those questions in one sitting. To be able to write it out and not have to face everyone's individual questions over and over was like taking those shattered pieces and slowly gluing them back together. Their responses filled us with the love, peace, and courage we needed to face the road ahead. To have people close to us in our corner praying for us, standing with us, and encouraging our every little step, slowly built us back up. Choosing to believe God was with us, in and through it all, allowed us to be able to breathe and keep taking the necessary steps forward.

The process took us a little over a year to get started and into the throes of it all. Our options were to try a few rounds of IUI (intrauterine insemination-a.k.a. the "turkey baster" method) then move on to IVF (in vitro fertilization- a.k.a. "the petri dish" method) if the IUI attempts were unsuccessful. Surely, IUI would work, and we wouldn't need to even cross into the IVF territory, we told ourselves.

As I moved into each phase of our preparation, I realized I needed to reach beyond our little group. There was a pleading within me—a need to express all I was experiencing in a real, raw way on a regular basis. My husband is much more private than I am, and he wasn't keen on letting any more people into our infertility world than already knew. So, convincing him I needed an outside outlet was tough. Eventually, he came to understand that he and I are wired very differently in that regard. He finally supported my decision to create a space where I could document every emotion and all the moments we were going through without judgment or fear. My account For the Love of Mom Genes on Instagram was born. It became an "Instablog" of sorts because pictures and little excerpts have always been easier for me than long drawn-out blog posts.

Letting people in on our journey was imperative to me as we moved forward. It doesn't mean it made the pain any less or the journey any easier, but it did lift some of the burden and allowed us to start crawling again. The infertility ride - and it is a ride - can be a lonely place to find yourself. It's a rollercoaster of ups and downs, twists and turns, extreme highs and lows, and several loops. Until you have been on that ride yourself, it is a very hard concept to grasp. To have people in our corner, from all corners of the world, sharing their stories of similar places in their own journeys was amazing. Slowly my loneliness started to dissipate.

In the months that followed we experienced tons of support from family and friends. We shared thousands of tears. We were given a team of incredible doctors and nurses. We spent way more money than we would have ever imagined. I endured hundreds of needles, scans, and dates with "Wanda" (the intravaginal ultrasound machine). We pushed through one canceled IUI, one failed IUI, one egg retrieval, 14 fertilized embryos, and five embryos that made it to the frozen stage. After one IVF frozen transfer (FET) of two embryos, we were blessed with twin girls. Our "Twirls."

God is good. All the time. Although I'd never imagined becoming a mommy through science, I'm truly grateful this is part of our story. God broke us all the way down to where He could be the only one to carry us through. He allowed us to experience and endure every high and low, twist and turn, needle and scan, poke and prod, all for His glory. He was, and is, able to be glorified through it all via our lives and our Instagram; the platform He created and continues to use. It is so mind-boggling.

BUT WAIT. He wasn't done.

Just when we'd started to approach the topic of trying again, (we weren't quite ready just yet, we told ourselves. Maybe in a few months' time, we thought. Once the girls turn one, we reasoned, we would consider starting the process over again) we were hit with a wonderful surprise.

We'd been told our chances of getting pregnant naturally were slim to none. The thought that I could be pregnant never crossed our minds when I started to feel like junk, and my clothes (that I just started to fit in again!) started becoming snug. About eight weeks into these unexplained symptoms and several pregnancy tests later (which I swore were just defective), it was confirmed via a legitimate blood test that yes, I was indeed pregnant. Against all odds, the unthinkable had happened. I had become pregnant naturally. With a third girl!

(Did I mention I always thought I would be the mom of all boys? God has quite the sense of humor, doesn't He?)

This once infertile pin cushion with an empty womb is now experiencing mommahood from both methods of needles and natural. And, I wouldn't change a thing about the path I took to get here.

Angie Kutzer

THE MELT DOWN

There I sat, in the grocery store parking lot, suddenly incapable of driving and unable to remember which way to go to get home. Part of my brain had simply shut down. I knew my children were there with me, buckled in and safe, but other than that my mind was completely blank. I picked up my cell phone and called the number saved as I.C.E (In Case of Emergency). My husband answered. I recognized his voice and said, "I don't know where I am. I don't know anything! The kids are with me, and I am scared!"

Somehow, my husband got enough information out of me to determine where I was. He picked up the kids and me safely and then drove me - confused and disoriented - to the nearest emergency room.

There, I was diagnosed as having temporary amnesia caused by stress. No real surprise there, not about the stress part anyway. But what about the temporary amnesia? Was I really so stressed I could forget most details of my daily life? The answer was YES. Yes, I was that stressed, and I was doing it to myself.

Amid motherhood, I had not been considering my health or well-being at all. I was so lost in the obsession to be all the mommy magazines said I should be, I completely missed the pulls at my heartstrings to be the mommy I was meant to be. And that is how my stress level got so elevated I ended up in the hospital, unable to remember anything.

After resting a while in the hospital, I sat and tried to re-member the events that led me to this point. The kids and I had gone to the library for toddler time. I remembered pack-ing the organic drinks and snacks, hand wipes, hand sanitizer, and our own blanket to sit on. (Wouldn't want to sit on the germ-infested library floor.) My load of "necessities" had looked more like the luggage for a family of 6 on a 2-week va-cation! When we left the library and got out to our van, I recalled sanitizing the baby while he screamed. Then sanitiz-ing the toddler while he squirmed. And then sanitizing the stroller while I loaded it. Finally, I loaded myself into the minivan, exhausted and sweaty.

Our next stop had been the grocery store. Oh, the dreaded grocery store. Once we arrived and parked, I proceeded to get out the blanket to cover all exposed metal that the baby would touch on the cart, the wipes to wipe the cart, the cart handle cover (which covered the handle I had already sanitized, mind you), and more. The toddler had walked beside me, holding my hand the entire time we were shopping (as if it's easy to shop while holding a toddler in one hand and pushing a cart, keeping a baby occupied, and pulling things off the shelves with the other), because I certainly didn't want him to touch anything "germy" while in the store. I remembered we had completed the daunting task of getting groceries and, at checkout, I had declined the sucker for the toddler, because duh, it had certainly been touched by too many people. Then, back out to our minivan we went. I loaded the kids and the groceries, disinfected the kids, disinfected myself, took all protective covers off the cart, and bagged them into the "need to wash" bag.

UGGH! That sounded exhausting as I replayed it in my mind! I was a wreck. Why was I doing this to myself every day?

I then remembered plopping into the van, sweaty again, and ready for bedtime. I recalled thinking: *It must be almost the end of the day*, relieved my husband would soon be home to take over for a bit. Then I remembered I had looked at the clock. It was only 11:30. A.M. Then I frantically thought: *I'm too exhausted to move! How will I make it another 5 hours?* Then, the panic began to set in about lunchtime. I remember thinking: *I haven't planned anything for lunch! We are not even home yet, and the kids will be starving and screaming soon!*

That was the last straw. I freaked out. And that is the last thing I remembered before ending up at the hospital.

There I lay in my hospital room, wondering what about this particular morning had pushed me over the edge. Sure, it was a rough morning, but no different than most. What about to-day had triggered this odd medical issue? Suddenly, the memory of the events of the tumultuous evening before came rushing back.

I had picked up my toddler and baby from my mother-in-law's house. While there, she had looked me straight in the eye and said: "Angie, you need to calm down or you are not going to be okay." I was so taken aback. How dare she tell me to calm down? *Who makes her an expert on what is best for my kids or me?* (She raised 3, mind you.)

The kids and I had gone home from there, and everything that could go wrong that evening had. I stressed about the baby crawling on the floor because it hadn't been swept that day. I disinfected all the toys and the bottles. I sleepily walked through the bedtime feedings and routines. In fact, I recalled how, in bed last night, with my husband next to me, I told him the story about what his mother had said to me, and shared just how disgusted I was that she felt it was okay to say that. He replied, "She's right, Angie, you're not going to make it to our kids' graduations if you keep up like this."

Holy Moly! Had he really just said that to me? My husband, my partner in this life, the man who is always supposed to have my back, had just sided with his mother? I was infuriated! I recalled yelling a bunch of tired, angry nonsense at him. But what I remembered most clearly is laying there after my husband had fallen asleep. As tears rolled down my face I thought: *Maybe they're right... I do feel overwhelmed and exhausted all the time. Am I even enjoying this blessing called motherhood? If the truth be told: not really. It's too much work.* As the tears continued to flow down my cheeks, I recalled praying: "Lord, please lead me to a more peaceful, enjoyable place in this lifelong commitment called motherhood." And I had fallen asleep in prayer.

In the silence and loneliness of that hospital room, I realized they had been right. The two people who loved me enough to tell me the truth, even though they risked my wrath had been right. I could see now how much I'd changed since becoming a mother. From the moment I found out about my first pregnancy, I adopted the outlook that everything was going to be perfect. The perfect children, the perfect house, the perfect food, the perfect plan to fight germs, and on and on. The perfect pictures in my mind were unattainable, but I had tried so hard anyway.

Once I had children, I very quickly found myself obsessed with the security of my children in every way and in every moment of every day. I regularly annoyed visitors with the thorough hand wash rule, declined strangers' requests to touch my babies, and disinfected everything. These rules and guidelines I had set forth for my family to live by had been breaking me. The pressure to strive for the perfect life and perfect health and perfect, well, everything; was too much to handle. My mommy brain had been on overdrive every moment, for years. So, there I sat, in the hospital, regaining my strength and my right mind.

Motherhood is an amazing, overwhelming, heart-wrenching, unexplainable blessing, and the most difficult 'job' in life, because it never ends. In this moment of clarity, I realized that throughout my short journey of motherhood I'd had too many moments of stress caused by my own faulty expectations of what it meant to be a good mother. I had been amped up way too high by my 24/7 job as germ patrol. I had become exhausted by the task of becoming an organic homemade baby food chef and overwhelmed by my need to become a safe products researcher. I had been on high alert every second of every single day. I was overprotective, overbearing, overworked and over-stressed.

Right there in the hospital room, I thanked God as loudly as my worn-out self could. "Thank you, Lord! Thank you for this opportunity to walk away from this, okay, but finally with my eyes wide open to the mistaken ways I have been going about motherhood. Thank you for blessing me with this clarity!" If I hadn't been blessed with temporary amnesia that day, I don't know if I would have survived motherhood.

Thankfully, I'm now able to see that my family deserves so much more than mama moodiness, frequent tense times, frazzled days, and impatient responses. My mother-in-law and my husband had been incredibly correct. And once I saw what they saw, I never looked back.

The years pass by way too quickly to fret about every little detail. The enjoyable parts of being a mom far outweigh stressful decisions and overwhelming moments. In retrospect, I can now see what matters most to me is that I show my boys love every single day. That we raise them with understanding and guidelines (not concrete walls). That we instill in them values and faith. And, that our boys can trust and rely on us always. Everything else I stressed about back then has no value at all.

Robin Stearns Lee

AM I STILL YOUR MOTHER?

The rocking chair is now relegated to a corner in the guest bedroom. Its wicker ties are frayed, and the cushioned seat is flattened. It was there when I nursed my youngest child and rocked all six of my grandchildren to sleep. It's too fragile for guest seating now, but I can't yet part with it.

I sit in that old rocker occasionally and remember. Remember a time when my lap was the best place to be, the late-night comfort it provided a fussy baby. Remember the story books read there. It was the best place to sit and read our favorite book – P.D. Eastman's *Are You My Mother?*

My copy of the book has a broken spine, teeth marks on the corner, crayon scribbles, and ripped pages. It was loved hard. I think I still have the words memorized, and I laugh when I remember how we physically jumped when reading the part where the mother bird's egg jumped and jumped. Every time.

Whatever child I was holding would snuggle closer as we read about the egg ready to hatch, the mother bird flying off to find him a juicy worm for his arrival, and the hatchling on a search for his mother. My child was secure in the whereabouts of his own mother, while the poor baby bird had to question a kitten, a hen, a dog and a SNORT, asking over and over again: "Are YOU my mother?"

This book has even managed to cement itself into our family vernacular. Once, I picked up my teenage son at football practice after getting my hair permed. The coach had to call for him several times as I stood at the gymnasium door waiting for him. My son had looked toward the door at each summons but didn't see me. Finally, I called out his name. When he came to the door, he took one look at my curly-tight short hair and said, "Who ARE you? You are not my mother!" He definitely knew who his mother was and who she wasn't.

Another time, I witnessed my toddler absently crawling into the lap of a lady sitting near me, who looked a bit like me. He looked up and quickly realized it was not me, and scampered off her lap. So, it couldn't be just any mother they needed. It was THEIR mother they wanted. It was me. I always tell anyone who will listen that those were my best days. Being home with the young children, having the freedom as a woman to choose to be home rather than working, greeting them after their naps, hearing their first words, reading them book after book after book.

Those years flew by. My children know where their mother is now, but they no longer need her. Well, they no longer need her in the same way they once did. What do I do with these mothering skills now, after the kids are grown and on their own?

That seems to be the most difficult part of mothering for me. Sure, it was hard when they were toddlers; when I was exhausted from chasing after them, protecting them, keeping them clean and well-fed. And who would ever want to re-live the teen years, when I felt like a warden, making sure they were still in their bed at night, and home at their designated curfew time. But now that they are grown, and that invisible line has been crossed between needy child and independent adult, it's hard to know how to parent.

I have had to learn to listen and not speak; to advise only when asked, to refrain from interfering. That has been hard. To see a possible train wreck about to happen and keep myself from speaking. That is very hard. I have to trust that I raised them right, that they will fall back on those timeless directives from their mother, and that I need to let them fly out of the nest alone.

It's at that point when the mothering job changes. "You can do it" replaces "Don't do that." "That sounds like a good idea" instead of "No, you can't." How do you turn it off? That mothering voice? You spent 18 to 20 years telling them what to do, and now must only be an on-call advisor.

When the grandchildren came along, that helped. I could become the fun grandmother! No longer responsible for a child's every move, I could do all the fun things with them and leave the tough stuff to THEIR mother. It is a blessing to still find a listening ear when you want to steer a young person right in life. Refreshing to find that the grandchildren WILL listen in a way their parents did not.

Not only has my role switched from full-time mother to an on-call advisor mother and grandmother, I find I am trying to also be a guide to my own mother as she is heading toward her elderly years. I feel free to tell her what to do, and I am surprised when she resists. I'm still trying to be someone's mother, ANYONE's mother, and my help is no longer welcome.

Mothering is a tough business. Having all the answers right at your fingertips no matter what issue your child encounters is exhausting. At this time of my life, I should be fondly remembering those mothering days, but grateful I no longer have to live them. I do feel glad when I am in the grocery store or a restaurant and see a child having a tantrum in front of their embarrassed parents. I can walk away with a smile, feeling fortunate I do not have to fix that situation. I can go home to my quiet house, where my things are lying just where I left them. Where the food I purchased is still in the refrigerator, not wolfed down by hungry teenage boys.

My memories are huge blessings. Much of mothering has been great fun, but I have a new phase of life ahead of me. The occasional phone calls still come. "Mom, what should I do about ....?" I smile, take a breath, and give the advice freely. Once asked, I can state my opinion. They do still need me, but it's a different quality of need now. And when they call, I can give the advice and then sleep well that night. It's their problem really, not mine. Their worries do not have to necessarily consume me anymore.

I am teaching myself to enjoy this new phase and not worry about what I can no longer do. Visits and calls with my children can be focused on sharing my new adventures, and hearing their stories. I can enjoy telling my grandchildren, "Let me tell you what YOUR dad did when he was your age!" Getting older is learning tolerance, learning what is no longer my business, and focusing only on what I can change within my own attitudes and thoughts. It has been a freeing experience.

I did my job, and I think I did it well. I've had some do-over time with grandchildren to guide and mold. And I am blessed to still have my own mother, who I can call and ask "How did you handle this when you were my age?" I can experience how she reacts to me in each phase of my life, and decide how I will do the same with my children.

At the end of *Are You My Mother?*, there is a full-page illustration of the baby bird with a frustrated look on his face and his little wings on his hips. He knows he has a mother and simply cannot find her. He also knows he is not able to get what he needs from a kitten, a hen, a dog or a SNORT. He needs his mother. Just like my children need me, and will always need me. As long as I am alive, and even long after, I will always be their mother.

Allison Mayfield Herrin

NO. MATTER. WHAT.

Oh, so many times I wanted to give up because it was too hard. I want to give up now, even as I write. I am convinced that even as you read this very sentence months or years from now, I will want to give up, because here's the thing: solo parenting will never stop being hard. It will never stop being the opposite of God's greatest plan for my kids. For your kids. We were never meant to do it alone. Kids were always meant to have two parents.

Single motherhood is infinitely harder, sometimes mind-numbingly painful, but just as beautiful. Sometimes, though, I have to look a little harder to find the beauty in all the chaos; the splendor in all the pain; the lessons in all the madness. Every day comes with the challenge of choosing to carry on.

I used to think I couldn't do hard things. I would crumble at the pressure. I was so self-centered and weak. On the outside, I was confident and strong; bold and sassy. Then, in an instant, I was side-swiped by humility. God gave me three little boys who needed me and had complete dependence on me. I didn't even know how to pay my bills on time or stick with one guy for very long. But in no time, not only did I become responsible for poop and puke and pacifiers, but for character building, heart mending and so much more. ME? My mind would go back to the same question over and over: How the hell am I going to do any of this? I can't! I don't even want to! I have to? WTF?!?! (Don't judge, if we can't be honest and real then none of this matters anyway.)

Oh God, I just knew I was going to fail miserably. At everything.

It took me years to learn to relax and trust the process. To not judge myself (or others) so quickly and so harshly. But I didn't get to that point easily. It used to be that any time things didn't go my way, I stressed. I mean I S.T.R.E.S.S.E.D! I can't tell you how many heads I took off with the stroke of my tongue. Stress made me nasty. But for the sake of my kids and my own sanity, I had to learn to trust the path that God had me on and look for the lessons during some really tough experiences. Otherwise, I was going to stress myself, and others, to death.

One of my most memorable lessons came one Christmas. It was the faith test of all faith tests. It was by far one of the hardest moments with my kids up to that point. But I had a choice, let the situation beat me or learn from it.

It was Christmas 2005. Not the first hard one but, by far, the hardest of all. We all know that the anticipation of Christmas through the eyes of our children is one of the greatest gifts there is. There is something magical about it. I always made sure my children knew the real meaning of Christmas, but I was looking forward to their wide-eyed anticipation as any other mother would be. Christmastime held a few of the precious fond memories I have of my childhood. As a mama, I was determined my children would have more than I did.

Unfortunately, this year had been a particularly tough one. I had been a single parent for almost three years and things were not getting any easier. I was still well below the poverty line and could barely put food on the table, much less consider Christmas gifts for my children. Our gift that year would be a warm house with electricity, and if we were really blessed, we might have a roast to go with the macaroni and cheese dinner that had become so familiar.

Christmas Day was approaching fast and my kids were still little. I hoped and even prayed that my children wouldn't notice its coming and going. That way, I wouldn't have to tell them. I could garner more time to make next year the best Christmas yet. The world wouldn't have it however. Christmas was everywhere and I couldn't escape it. I knew I had to tell them.

"Cameron, I need to talk to you." My voice cracked as I prepared to devastate my eight-year-old son. (My other two boys were too young to know any different, so I focused on him.) With his list in my hand, and through shame-filled tears of a mom who desperately wanted to create cherished childhood memories for my son but had failed, I began: "I know you are asking Santa for these things this year but I need to tell you the truth. There is no Santa. I am Santa and it's been a rough year, and..."

I couldn't finish. It was too much. My kids had been through so much. Why God? Why did I have to disappoint them like this, too?

Cameron sat there silently while I composed myself enough to ask him, "How do you feel?" To which he responded

"I feel fine, I'm just curious how you did it all those other years. We've had some pretty great Christmases."

Stunned is the only word I can use to describe my reaction. In comparison to the rest of the world, I thought our Christmases had stunk, but he wasn't comparing us to the rest of the world. He was content.

And so, the years have passed, and Santa Clause has not become a part of our family celebrations. Our circumstances forced us to celebrate that Christmas in a humble and meager fashion, yet not nearly as humble as the day Christmas came in to existence; the day our Savior was born into the humblest of circumstances. And that's what we began to focus on. What was sacrificially given to us, not what we could get.

That day, so many years ago, I thought I was tarnishing traditions and childhood memories; ruining their chance to be like everyone else. That Christmas, when there were no gifts under the tree, I discovered we were given the best Christmas gift yet: we were given the chance to worship a Savior without the distraction of commercialism. I had bought the lie that material things would make us happy. Our circumstances through the eyes of my son, proved I was wrong.

So yes, being a single mama comes with many challenges. It's rough when I'm in the middle of some really, really hard things, but it has made me trust less in myself and to trust His process, His journey for me as a single mama instead. So many times, I asked the question: *Why?* So many times, I wanted clarity: *Why God? Help me understand.* But then, I read something by Mother Teresa where she told a fellow servant that she would not pray for clarity. She said she had never had clarity about anything but chose to trust anyway. She said that clarity is something we cling to and it becomes our source of satisfaction rather than God himself. So today, like Mother

Teresa, my prayer is that I would not yearn for clarity or an answer to the question "why," but that I would learn to trust God in every season of my single-parenthood. No. Matter. What.

Vicky Willenberg

WHAT'S WRONG WITH FINE?

"You know what would be so cool, Mom?" my 10-year-old asked as we drove to music lessons. Without taking my eyes off the road, I raised my eyebrows and quirked my head in his direction to let him know I was ready to hear his fabulous idea.

"It would be so cool if someone invented a robot that drove kids to all their after-school activities!" He grinned at his self-perceived brilliance.

The "right" response would have been something along the lines of: "That's a great idea, buddy! You're so creative!" Unfortunately, I couldn't formulate the "right" response because of the dull roaring in my ears, signaling my head was preparing to explode. Instead, I came up with a different response. Turning my full gaze on his sweet face, I said (probably with more sarcasm than was appropriate,) "Uh, someone already did, buddy. It's called ME!"

Being somewhat fluent in sarcasm himself, my son wasn't the slightest bit put out by my response. He simply turned to me and said, "Well yeah, but at least the robot would be content doing it."

And that, my friends, is what you call a sucker punch to the gut. I stared at him just as I had the time he told me he loved hugging me because I was "so, so squishy" or when he informed me that Jack's house was the best house because his mom sits on the floor and plays Legos with them. Innocent words from an equally innocent source, who has no idea he just took a scalpel to my Achilles heel.

You could hear a pin drop for the remaining handful of minutes of our car ride. Him, obliviously watching the scenery fly by. Me, gripping the steering wheel until my knuckles were white and aching. A swift kiss on the cheek and he was out the door, leaving me alone to stew. He thinks I'm discontent. He's wrong- so, so wrong. I am not discontent. I'm fine. My life is fine. The season of motherhood I'm in is fine. As I sped off to the grocery store to grab the remaining ingredients I needed for dinner, my gut began to churn. The wheel of emotions was spinning until it came to a grinding halt, and landed squarely on a single feeling: guilt. I knew "Fine" was a terrible answer. The wheel began spinning again as I flew through the aisles of the grocery store, ever conscious of the ticking clock reminding me I had only minutes before I had to pick up my son from guitar lessons.

Guilt soon gave way to a myriad of other emotions: sadness, frustration, defensiveness, and finally anger. Through the self-checkout line and packing my reusable grocery bags in the car, my anger grew. Why was "fine" the wrong answer, anyway? Why was a "fine" life something to feel guilty or ashamed over? When had "fine" become synonymous with "ungrateful, unsatisfied, and discontent"? Why did "fine" now signal a problem?

The seasons of motherhood change quickly- despite what it may feel like while you're living it. Before you can blink, the babies who once kept you up all night with colicky cries become the teens who keep you up until you hear the key in the lock at curfew. Yet within those seasons, there are a million sunny days and stormy weeks. In this season of life, I have two active sons. At ten and thirteen, they have healthy social lives and a passion for music that fills every day of the week. They are well on their way to becoming their own people, separate from me. However, when the flurry of texts settles, it is me who must drive them to the movies to meet their friends and haul sound equipment to band rehearsal. I am the taxi driver and the cruise director. I am the permission slip signer, field trip chaperone, lunch packer, rule enforcer, chore reminder, and consequence deliverer.

A glimpse in the rearview mirror no longer shows the sweet toothy grin of a toddler or the dirty face of a first grader. Today's glimpse reflects back the crown of a head buried in a cell phone or the profile of a young man with his ever-present white earbud cord dripping from his ears. There are no more Cheerios or fishy crackers in the backseat, only discarded shoes and twenty-pound backpacks, all blanketed in the smell that can only be described as "adolescent boy." These days, we exist in a world of in-between. They are no longer little boys, delivering sugar-sweet kisses or asking for more of my time and attention. Every day they become less dependent on me to provide the things they need to feel safe and happy. At the same time, they are incapable of surviving on their own. They don't need me to supply the fun, just to drive them there and pick them up after that fun is finished.

My role is also in a constant state of flux during this season. I spent so many hours when they were little pouring into my children, preparing them to navigate a world much larger and fraught with more challenges than either of us even knew. I taught the important lessons and tried to give them the skills and tools to overcome obstacles and even admit defeat when necessary. Faith, hope, love, perseverance, kindness, humility, empathy, patience, and resourcefulness are the rocks upon which we built them up so we could one day send them out. While they are years from leaving the nest, they are venturing farther and farther out and, at times, barely visible in the distance. I am not the head coach in their lives any longer. I have been relegated to the sidelines, vigilantly standing guard. Sometimes I rush in to defend. Other times I maintain my position and can only cheer and encourage while they wage their own battles. It's not easy.

My new role is filled with beautiful highs and some pretty rough lows - often within the same 24-hour period. My job is not finished – far from it, in fact. My boys still need me and want me in their lives. They long for independence and wage war to make their opinions known, while surreptitiously glancing in my direction, looking for approval. Some days we do it all right. There's a perfect balance of give and take. Other days, not so much. But we are figuring it out together, as a family. And I'd say we are doing just fine.

Stephanie Haynes

THE THIN FRAYED EDGES OF MOTHERHOOD

When I first learned I was pregnant, I was devastated. Seriously. My husband and I had only been trying for one month. ONE month. I had been looking forward to the freedom of "trying," of living life on the proverbial "edge" (Sad, I know). All my life I'd been afraid to get pregnant and now, here I was ready for the season where doing what you do to get pregnant was totally okay without using any precautions, and it was already over?

But, as I had done with everything else in my life I took my pregnancy in stride and made my plan. I planned for when I would take my maternity leave. I planned for an in-house day-care. I even planned for what changes my body was going to go through and the development of my baby by reading *What to Expect When You're Expecting.* Not once did I think about preparing to be a parent. The thought never crossed my mind.

I guess I believed I would just know how to be a parent because I'd figured everything else out in my life up to that point. How could a baby be any different? (Feel free to laugh out loud at that last statement.) Never mind that the only baby I'd ever been around was my younger sister and she was only 22 months younger than me. Sure, I'd just figure it out.

Six years later: I had a daughter who was 5 and a son who was 18 months old and I, (understandably) was a wreck. I had no clue what I was doing as a parent, and it showed. I had a strong-willed daughter who ran all over me, and as a strong-willed child myself our battles were epic. My son was the sweetest, most compliant child ever, so he often got lost in the bickering that went on between my daughter and me. Because my parenting was a mess, I strove to fix it. All. The. Time. Which meant there was little or no energy left over for my husband, or anything else for that matter. My health was in shambles, my emotions were raw, and I just wanted to quit it all.

In utter desperation and sheer force of will (My mama did not raise a quitter y'all), I sought help. First from a personal counselor, who started speaking truth into my weary soul, and then from my local church who directed me to a mothers group called "Hannah's Circle."

Now understand, I'm not a joiner. And, I don't trust women. At least I didn't then. To walk into a group of other mamas was more intimidating and panic-inducing than standing naked in front of a group trying to give a speech. Really. I was terrified my massive imperfections would be judged, that I would be found to be a horrible mother and that I would be gossiped about in whispers in our church hallways and the grocery store. That's how most of my experiences with women had turned out; why would this group be any different?

And still, I chose to go. My desire to learn to parent my children better was greater than my fear of being condemned. I wanted to end the strife between my daughter and me, to give my children a life free of the chaos I had created.

I'm so glad I went.

The morning of the first Hannah's Circle was the starting point of a dramatically different trajectory for my children's lives as well as my own. I sat down next to a gorgeous young woman who introduced herself and shared that she had just moved to our town from another state, the very same state I had moved from not one year previously. Our leader was a gracious woman who shared her parenting battle scars with such rawness we were all in tears, touched by her vulnerability, but infused with her hope that her children, in God's hands, were protected. I knew I was in the place I was supposed to be. I knew I would receive the healing and transformation my children needed so I could be the mother I was created to be.

I met other women over the course of that semester. Real women who weren't afraid to be transparent and who didn't judge another mom for her shortcomings. Several of us formed a bond that, to this day, has never been replicated in my life. I believe it has something to do with the battleground we were on together; aside from the infant-toddler-preschool stage, we were all in, each of us experienced incredible tragedies and were fused together over them. Divorce, childhood diagnoses, panic and anxiety, insecurities due to mistreatment by loved ones, death; these were some of the life events we faced together.

We also celebrated the joys: birthdays, first steps, lost teeth, new babies, new jobs, and callings to serve in new ways. Our group gathered for all the holidays; most of us were transplants and had no family close by. We "weekended" together, creating our own Friday night Happy Hours on the beach where we lived. While this season was filled with its share of tragedy, all of it was overshadowed by the hope that together we could face anything.

And then came my turn to be transparent.

I sat in my bedroom, surrounded by these incredible women. We were holed away from our children, trying to have a Bible study. I don't remember quite how we got onto the subject of me, but the next thing I knew all eyes were focused on me as my gorgeous same-state friend said: "Stephanie, you cannot keep going on like this. You won't last. I know you love your children, but they need you to live differently."

The other women nodded and offered words of encouragement and support.

They listened for over an hour as my story slowly came out. My fears at being a failure, my struggles for perfection. My doubts at never being good enough.

Not once did they condemn. Not once did they ridicule or even utter ways I could be "fixed." Instead, they prayed and then stepped in.

Over the next three months, these women showed up to take my son to pre-school—both ways. They sent me encouragement over the phone. They watched my children. They loved on my daughter. They stood with me in the struggle to be undone only to be remade. They were Jesus in the flesh; loving me in ways I couldn't do for myself. It was the worst time of my parenting journey and the best. The worst because I had to lay down my expectations of what a good mother should be. This was a terrifying freefall that left me breathless in my uncertainty; would God show up?

Yes. Yes. Yes.

Being broken down was the best thing to ever happen to me. It forever changed my life and my children's lives. There had been screaming matches, threats, and things flung across rooms. There had been frustration and bitterness and insecurity. I hated being a mom. Had I stayed that way... I don't even want to think about how that would have affected my children. I am forever grateful for those women; those "other mommies" who stepped in to love my children as their own while they loved me through the healing and restoration that needed to come. Their love healed my children in ways I couldn't; healed us all.

Since then, my motherhood road has not been smooth (it never is, is it?) We have walked through homeschooling, long-distance moves, broken hearts, broken curfews, broken spirits and broken promises. We have celebrated black belts and soccer goals and acceptance letters and driver's licenses and first jobs.

Through it all, the fears of failure, the struggle to be perfect, and the condemnation of "not good enough" have raged at the door of my heart, but these women, with their love and acceptance, forever locked it shut. I have made huge mistakes. I have regrets and "If only..." moments. But all of them are now covered by God's grace, the grace He first showed me through a band of other moms who were with me on the thin, frayed edges of motherhood.

Lara Busold

THE FEAR IS REAL

I glanced out the front window after hearing the school bus come to a stop. Our puppy wagged his tail with excitement. The familiar sound of the school bus indicated his favorite part of the day - when the kids started trickling home from school – had finally arrived. Moments later the door opened and my usually chipper third grader immediately fell into my arms and began to cry. I thought something terrible must have happened. My thoughts ranged from a bully to a trip to the principal's office, or possibly even an altercation with a friend. When she finally calmed down enough to speak, I asked her what had happened. "I'm in the spelling bee! I made it!" she sobbed. I thought this was something to celebrate, but we obviously were not on the same page.

Apparently, each of the third and fourth grade classes in her school had held classroom spelling bees that afternoon. The top two contestants from each class would then go on to compete in the school-wide spelling bee the following week. Well, much to her anguish, she had earned a spot as one of the top two contestants in her class, and now she wanted nothing to do with the school-wide spelling bee. "I tried to spell the words wrong, but I just couldn't do it!" It took a lot of self-control to keep my composure and not crack a smile or let a chuckle slip out. I had never witnessed anyone that upset with personal success!

Of course, I already knew she was not upset about spelling words correctly. Rather her fears stemmed from thoughts of standing in front of hundreds of teachers, administrators, parents, and fellow students at the spelling bee. Understandable. Her initial response, and her continued response up until the day before the spelling bee, was to give up her position in the contest. After all, there were plenty of other kids who actually wanted to participate.

But, as any experienced parent would advise, this was a classic teachable moment. My husband and I knew we needed to encourage her to confront her fears and overcome this challenge. Thankfully, my daughter was blessed with a wonderful teacher who shared our sentiments. Her teacher saw the value in letting students find courage in a safe, yet daunting contest such as the spelling bee. She told our daughter she could decide, right up until the day of the spelling bee, whether she would participate. We certainly were not going to force her, but there would be steady and persistent doses of encouragement in the days to follow.

The day finally had arrived. After much prayer, Bible verse recitation, motivation, debate, and promise of celebratory activities to follow, she bravely decided to participate in the spelling bee. We arrived at her elementary school right on time. She joined her fellow participants on the stage in the gym while my husband and I filed into the stands. She was nervous, of course. So was I. It was hard to not notice the grimaced look on her face and her incessant clock-watching increasing by the minute. My thoughts raced as I sat there watching her struggle: What if she got up to the microphone and couldn't speak, or lost control of some sort of bodily fluid, or spelled a word wrong? What if we encouraged her to do this, and something dreadfully embarrassing happened? She will never forgive us, and we will never forgive ourselves! Thankfully, God brought to my attention the numerous Bible verses about overcoming fear that I had imparted to her over the last week. I felt His mercy sooth my anxious, mother's heart. I prayed He would soothe her precious heart too.

As the spelling bee participants moved through the line, spelling their assigned words one by one, some filtered to the next round while others hoped to get a chance to try again next year. My little girl inched closer and closer to the microphone. Her body language screamed anxiety. She told me later she could not stop shaking. I wanted to rescue her, but knew she had to do it. She spelled her first word correctly. Her quivering voice was barely audible, but she made it through to the next round. Actually, she made it to the third round and then gladly participated in the remainder of the event as a spectator. Her loss did not matter to her or to us. Her success had nothing to do with how far she had progressed in the competition, or the words she did or did not spell correctly. Her success had everything to do with proving to herself she could face and overcome her fears.

Our family celebrated her bravery with lots of hugs and kisses and ice cream that evening. She received hugs and encouragement from her wonderfully supportive teacher and high-fives from her friends. She basked in her moment, overcome with equal doses of pride and relief.

I realize this spelling bee is such a relatively small event in my daughter's life, and I can almost guarantee she will face much greater challenges in her future. As her mom, I would love to promise her (and myself) that she won't ever have to face difficult circumstances. But, she will never discover who she was created to be—or who she was created to depend on—if I don't encourage her to embrace challenges.

I know God longs to rescue us in the same way I wanted to rescue my daughter as she stood on that stage shaking and gripped with fear. He sees our struggles. And He waits. He waits for us to ask for His comfort. I can only imagine the joy He experiences when we open our hearts to His peace. God doesn't promise us we won't face hardships, but He does promise to bear our burdens. He will soothe our anxious hearts. He will give us the courage to be all He created us to be. He longs to show us His glory. God doesn't measure our success according to the number of challenges we endure. He doesn't even care if we fail. Godly success is measured according to the number of times we surrender our struggles to Him—and He receives the glory. I pray my daughter will seek His peace throughout her life, no matter how important or insignificant a circumstance may seem. I pray she will strive for Godly success—and He will receive the glory.

Kimberly Ritter

FOREVER MOTHER'S DAY

Mother's Day holds many mixed emotions for me. Growing up, I always enjoyed celebrating it with my mother. She would spend days with the other women of our church preparing a special Mother's Day celebration feast at our church, which meant preparing a large amount of everything. She would rise early on Mother's Day to get to church on time to set up, so she could enjoy having all her extended family in one place in celebration of mothers and grandmothers. Her joy on this special day came from preparing with love favorite meals for others.

As a child, I dreamed of my own Mother's Days, complete with the life of the white picket fence, marrying my Prince Charming and having lots of children. Oh, and I can't forget the dog, well maybe two dogs. That dream didn't come true the way I thought it would. Let's face it, Cinderella is a fairytale, right?

Today my Mother's Days are spent with three wonderful "bonus" sons, (thanks to my loving and devoted husband), a daughter-in-love, and four fabulous grandchildren who are funny, bright, smart and unbelievably thoughtful. And yes, I have the two dogs.

There is much pain squeezed in between those paragraphs, however. For years, I dreaded Mother's Day because it is one of the most difficult holidays when you have no children. My Mother's Days were once filled with anger, bitterness, and resentment. I began skipping Mother's Day Sunday at church because they always asked for the mothers in the congregation to stand and be honored. I stayed seated with regret, anger, and resentment; resentment for even attending that day. Resentment because I never gave birth to my children. Resentment at not having my children with me to watch them grow up, to hear their laughter, to see their smiles and adore those memories. Resentment for not having their baby scent engraved into my memory as only a mother would have. I would never take walks with them on the beach or teach them to boogie board in the ocean. I would never nurture them back to health after an illness or kiss their boo-boos and put on a Superman Band-Aid. I would never have the opportunity to tell them about Jesus and how much God loves them. No Easters, no birthday celebrations, no sports, no graduations, no weddings.

It took some time, but healing has come. The anger and resentment have been laid at the cross for it is no longer my burden to bear. Now in church on Mother's Day, I stand because I know I AM a mother. I know that once my children were conceived in my womb, I became a mother and nothing can take that away from me. (Jeremiah 1:5: Before I formed you in the womb I knew you, before you were born I set you apart.) I know my children were created and even though they never made it to earth I know they are in Heaven. My children never felt pain; they never felt fear nor turmoil. They were never bullied or disappointed. They were never sick. They never saw death, only life – eternal life. (John 3:16: For God so loved the world that He gave His only son that whosoever believeth in Him shall not perish but have eternal life.) I know my children are seated with Jesus. He is reading to them and loving them only the way God can love. They are playing as children play, and I hear their laughter. I see them running and playing and I see their faces beaming with smiles so vibrant. They are healthy and full of life.

Even though the tears stream down my face while I have this vision, my heart is filled with complete excitement and joy knowing I will join them one day and that day will be my forever Mother's Day. That day will be filled with the love and excitement and joy my mother felt on Mother's Day for years as she worked so hard preparing for all her family to be together. That day it will be my turn to read to them, to walk on the beach with them and touch them. Oh, to touch them! How I long for that moment. It will be a day of reuniting and experiencing the love I so desire – the love only a mother can have from her children - and every day will be Mother's Day for I will be with my children.

Betts Keating

WE ARE MOTHERS

Recently, I watched Steel Magnolias. It's one of my all-time favorites. As a writer, I love to let every single well-written word of that movie wash over me. It is like music to my ears. And while each character has their own shining moment of eloquence, none shines more brightly for me than M'Lynn's graveside soliloquy. The scene depicts a mother who has just lost her daughter. We watch as she rides waves of emotions without so much as a moment in between to catch her breath before the next wave collapses onto her. First a wave of anger, then fear, rage, and finally grief. Through her tears, she explains how she was supposed to die first. She has always been prepared to go first. Children are never supposed to die before their parents.

I'm nothing like M'Lynn in that I've never lost a child. At least, not yet. What I do understand about M'Lynn's battle is the scars hidden beneath her anguish. I fully understand as a mother what it's like to fight for your child while she is still living, hoping and praying it will be enough. That you will be enough to be sure you're never the one standing at the grave-side of your child.

When I submitted my application to the mother/daughter online matching service, I had no idea what to expect. I felt I was a relatively experienced care-giver. I had helped take care of my much younger brother and sister, I'd purchased my first car with money I had earned babysitting, and I'd even worked multiple summers as a camp counselor. I never ex-pected the challenges that came along with the daughter I would be matched with would almost break me.

I don't think M'Lynn expected her trip down motherhood lane was going to be quite so difficult either. She may not have expected it, but because of it she became a force to be reck-oned with. You can see it in the moment she holds Shelby's face and forces her to "Drink the juice!" Every battle she fought was a desperate attempt to keep her daughter alive. Every time she dug in and became stubborn, insisting on Shelby's cooperation, it was out of a need to protect her. There is never a time in the movie where she is not com-pletely in tune with Shelby's mood, her countenance, and her health. And there is never a time she is not aware that Shelby is walking a delicate tightrope between life and death. Her mothership sonar is on high alert the entire movie.

When my youngest daughter was born with a congenital heart defect I, too, became a force to be reckoned with. I, too, have a mothership sonar that never completely turns off. The best way I can describe it is the feeling of standing on shifting sand. It's unsteady. It requires constant correction and strong balance, even when my feet are in perpetual movement. The challenge of staying on your feet when all you really want to do is collapse never ends. Just when I think I've "pulled myself together" something happens to throw a kink into my sanity.

It happened again just the other day. It was a regular weekday, during a regular week, while I was probably doing something regular (like dishes, or laundry, or sitting around all day watching TV and eating chocolate). I got a phone call from my youngest daughter's school. This was only a slightly unusual occurrence. I've received those kinds of calls before. You can't send your kid to school and not expect the usual run of viruses. She's had them all. Other than spending an exorbitant amount of time in doctor's offices, she's a very normal kid. She has regular childhood illnesses, only she gets them more often than most. But, hey, a cold or a stomach virus is nothing in comparison to a heart condition. And usually, on those kinds of days, it's already obvious by her appearance in the morning. Either she's just not quite herself, or a bit lethargic maybe, but on those days, I have time to prepare myself for the possibility of a phone call and an early pick-up.

But the morning before this call, she was fine. Exceptional really, considering everything she endures. For all intents and purposes, she is totally healthy… except for that annoying little thing called a heart condition. So, when I looked down and saw the name of the school appear on my phone, my mind went blank. My knees buckled. I could barely breathe and my pulse raced. Why? Why today of all days does a phone call from my daughter's school send me to "that place?" My "normal" was interrupted. My "peace" was invaded. My "wisdom" was jarred. My heart was broken. Re-broken. And it takes time to for it to heal. It just takes time. Thankfully, the phone call was nothing. It wasn't even a live person. It was an automated message about an upcoming school holiday. So how exactly… why exactly… what exactly happened to me?

There really is no limit to the effects of trauma and grief on human psyche. Especially when you're a mom and it involves your kid. I am never able to predict how far out it will drag me, until it's too late and I find myself in the middle of an ocean of fear without a flotation device. Even someone like me, who has done relatively well weathering the storms, can experience a gut-wrenching flashback with absolutely no warning. That day, my brain completely and utterly believed I was about to receive bad news and my body had a very real physical reaction to it. It was a dirty trick, but I can see it was also my brain's way of releasing stress and anxiety. Every time I have an "episode," it's one more opportunity to unload the residual effects of the pain. Every time, I leave another piece of it behind. Every time, it leaves me stronger and re-solved to fight harder for my daughter's very life.

When she stood at Shelby's graveside, M'Lynn's heart had not healed yet either. She was still in fight mode, even though the person she had spent her whole life fighting for was gone. She was still desperate to "save" Shelby. It's an instinct that cannot be turned off, especially if you are used to fighting every minute of every day for your child. Especially if you fight daily to continue to believe that your daily fight will somehow matter, that somehow you can heal or fix the chronic.

Like M'Lynn, I didn't ask for the fight. It found me. It be-came part of my game plan for caring for my daughter the moment I gave birth. The moment I became a mother. And not just any mother. The moment I became her mother. The mother/daughter online matching agency scoured the entire universe for the right candidate, the best soldier, the right mother for my daughter. I was the best choice of all the appli-cants. I had the perfect qualifications. The job belonged to me and only me from the beginning. It took me forever to realize, but M'Lynn and I are the ones uniquely qualified for our roles. We were given the task. We are mothers.

Tiffany Pate

YOU'LL JUST KNOW?

"Oh, you'll just know," she said, patting my hand softly. Her voice had that tone that speaks of a million stepped-on Legos, years of early morning whispers in rocking chairs, and restless nights waiting for teenagers to return home. Every wrinkle and laugh line in her face told a story, and it was a story grounded in her experience and reflected in her confidence. I desperately wanted to soak in every word. I wanted to hold on to that sentence like a two-year-old clutches her old weathered blanket, but I knew I couldn't. Not that her words didn't hold truth, but for me they shattered my motherhood.

I've heard it before, and I've felt it before. I've seen those words dance around mommy circles on the lips of other women. You begin to hear it around baby number two, when the cups of coffee are always cold and the same pair of yoga pants are worn for more than two days in a row. Someone is standing and swaying with a baby on their hip while toddlers, in various stages of undress, run through the kitchen in packs. That's when the question comes up: Are you done? "Done" always means are you done with maternity pants, sleepless nights, the mysterious stains on every article of clothing you own, and the never-ending supply of sour sippy cups under the car seats. The question is always met with a sideways laugh, a few sleep-deprivation jokes, and then with the same statement:

You will just know; your family will just feel finished.

The other moms nod their heads in quiet agreement. Like they all received the same mommy manual I somehow didn't get. The one, where somewhere between "How to Get Your Child to Sleep Through the Night" and "An Ode to Leggings," there is a chapter on "Being Finished."

"You'll just know" seems to be a banner they all gather under, smiling and joyful, while for me it lands heavy on my shoulders, like a dark gray, wool pea coat that is two sizes too big. Warm and caring, yet smothering, heavy, and almost crushing at the same time. It makes me wonder if my manual just got lost in the mail? Or, maybe, because motherhood and I didn't start off on the right foot, I was never going to get one?

It seems like forever ago, yet hurts like it was just yesterday. Just yesterday when two pink lines popped up on a test. Just yesterday when the day blurred into a haze of grocery store runs, too many glasses of water, about seven more pregnancy tests, and tears streaming down my face while sitting in a Mother's Day church service. Like a perfect storybook beginning, our first Mother's Day as a married couple was met with a total of 16 little pink lines.

But like any story, nothing is perfect. Two weeks later, as I tossed and turned through nightmares, I woke covered in sweat, doubled over in pain, losing our first child. A gut-wrenching yet numb feeling settled in me, deep in me, as I sat on the paper cover of the exam table. Praying, weeping, wishing, yet terrified to have hope. The day when we were supposed to see our tiny little one for the first time on the hospital's monitor was instead spent in a cold ER watching a silent womb. My lifeless womb. The silence didn't linger. It was instead quickly replaced with a gaping hole of pain where this little voice would whisper fears and damnations with every pregnancy test in the months that followed. This little voice called out "You're missing it all. You're missing your baby." Missing the gentle kicks and belly jump hiccups. You're missing registries, baby cribs and unsolicited advice from strangers. You're missing your perfect Mother's Day-inspired fairy tale. You are going to miss it all because you aren't worthy."

But, I wasn't missing all of that for long. Soon a baby did come, and I shoved that whisper down into the little hole it crawled out of. I silenced it by focusing on finding my unsure footing in mommy life. Laundry, diapers, bottles, and late-night rocking chair marathons all fell into a rotating loop of motion where I had to succeed. I had to prove I had the right to be called "mom."

Exhausted, broken, and totally lifeless, I painted on my happy face every morning, peeling it off in a crumbled sob every night. Life kept going, and yet again, circled back around to two little pink lines. While we thought we were taking steps forward growing our family, we found out we were falling back yet again. Back into the whispers and accusations of unworthiness.

That set of pink lines served to amplify the voice while nausea and exhaustion came in waves, creating a soothing white noise of: pregnant. Louder and louder the sounds of pregnancy echoed till one morning I woke up, suddenly with a calm stomach. Like a sudden break in the storm, there was nothing. No illness, no lack of energy, nothing. The voice started churning, over and over, while the pit in my heart grew and grew. I knew. I just knew. Others tried to speak words of life and hope, but I knew. I was lifeless. Weeks went by, till one day the voice was finally screaming as we stared at yet another motionless ultrasound monitor while a doctor whispered, "I'm sorry."

This time the voice told me: "You're missing." Those words refused to go down this time. This time it followed those words with: "You're a horrible, horrible mother." That voice rocked back and forth in my soul, screaming: "You didn't even know you'd lost your child. You're an awful mother, that's why this keeps happening. Your children are better off without you."

Those words played over and over in my head like a one-hit-wonder from the 80's, till their echo reverberated through every piece of my life. They imprinted themselves onto the DNA of my motherhood. Sometimes the song became a quiet melody, like elevator music where I could barely make out the tune. Other times, in the moments when I would meet someone and they asked, "How many kids do you have?" it would come back like a loud rock anthem screaming over my internal speakers: "You're missing. You're missing. You. Are. Missing!"

I am missing two little faces to keep clean. Two little sets of shoes that will never be lost. Two more sets of Christmas pictures to get every year. There are two missing places in our van, at our kitchen table, in our laps. There are two names that will never be written on backpacks for the first day of school.

Two little people's stuff I won't trip on every single day, no matter how many times I say it doesn't belong on the floor. There is this feeling of something more, something else, someone else, that should be around. But I shove it down. Struggling to manage the joys of my life with the sorrows of my soul.

Longing for those little missing faces, but realizing what it would mean to have them. Having those two faces would mean these little faces that currently stare at me from behind peanut butter sandwiches would vanish. It's a math problem that can never be solved, powered by guilt. Feelings of guilt for wishing for more. Feelings of guilt for the days I lose my temper and the voice sings out: "That's why they're missing. You couldn't have been their mom." Feelings of guilt for the days when I fall into a daydream, wondering what they would have looked like. Dreaming of what their voices would have sounded like when they called out "Mom!" only to have the dream quickly fade because one of my sons calls for me. Feeling guilty for longing for the swirls missing from the canvas that is my motherhood. It's a messy painting we started, but the years go on and we learn.

I've learned to settle into the missing, and let it be a part of my life. Let it root in and take up space, which creates in me a need to constantly check and count. Some call it OCD, I call it "mom life." There is a constant need to check for the missing. Check for keys, wallets, shoes, and counting of heads in a row. One, two, three. Three little people in my life all in a row, holding hands, smiling at me with sticky faces, ready for wherever we are going. Like the little baby ducks drawn in nursery books, they follow their mom through the rows at Target.

One, two, three.

One, two, three.

There's still something missing. Something missing because the count in my heart keeps going. One… two… three… four… five. *Five.*

I allow myself to take time to practice stopping at three. I gather up three piles of clothes on the floor, call out three reminders that shoes go in the closet and the constant reminder to flush the toilet. There is grocery shopping, breaking up fights, leading discussions on which is the better superhero (Batman or Superman) and doling out guidelines on self-hygiene.

We go to play dates and chat with other mommies. Mommies who bounce babies on their knees, or try desperately to find a comfortable spot for their pregnant selves to sit. We chat about opinions on the best bottles, wonder if cloth diapers are worth it, and discuss our favorite teachers. The cold coffee is passed around while the microwave beeps and the herd of toddlers take out something else in the other room. A quick prayer goes up that it wasn't your kid, and if it was yours, you pray it's in the budget to replace whatever they broke. Then, you brace yourself. You brace yourself for the mom sigh and the "Are you done?" conversation that always comes after crashes and crying kids.

"You'll just know," someone coos.

That's when I chug cold coffee, trying not to look over the top of my cup. Holding down whatever I can. You'll just know. It swirls around my soul, pushing and questioning everything I know to be true about my motherhood. But, I don't know. And I don't think I will ever really know because there are two tiny holes in my whole.

Maybe the answer lies somewhere in the missing manual? Maybe, between a chart of how many times it's safe to microwave cold coffee and a map on how to navigate the Lego land mines of a six-year-old, there's a space for the missing. A small space where words are messy, and perfect, and yet full of pain. A space where the story of being the mommy to an angel has a voice. Where it teaches you to smile through the questions and answer with honesty and gentleness. Where no matter how long your child was in your life, you can see them always in your heart. Where the feeling of forgetting something finally settles and you will just know. You will know that your family is finally complete, just temporarily separated.

Sandy Tyson

I HAVE SOMETHING TO SAY ABOUT MOTHERHOOD

The finest and most blessed purpose I have ever had was when I became Mom.

The wide-eyed young woman I once was had no idea what the future held but was excited and anxious to share the news with family and friends that she was with child. I was filled with joy at the news. In the days that followed, I would lay quietly, trying to feel the news inside my body, but could feel nothing yet.

My childhood experiences gave me doubts as to understanding myself, much less how to navigate this new title of "Mother." My childhood was full of hurt, fear, and abandonment, even though I had a mother, father and 3 older siblings in my home. I longed for a mother's face to gaze at, to touch, and to talk to, but those longings were met with little hope. I didn't have a mother-mentor to guide me in her early years so that I would have wisdom to apply when I had my own children. My sister was more caring toward me, but my brothers were more supportive of each other as we all tried to survive living in this unloving existence called "home."

My marriage was into its second year when I got the news I was pregnant. My husband and I were so excited to start a family. We saw it as an expression of our own love and devotion. The firstborn of our two children was a boy and I was in awe at the miracle of the gift he was to me. It was as if he came right from the heavens, placed in my arms, and I became "Mom."

There were no words to describe the feelings of love and blessing that came over me. I was profoundly moved by the sheer amount of innocence I was holding in those few precious moments after his birth. I knew without a doubt that this was a representation of God's lifetime love toward me, giving me the job of being a mother. I knew this job was important (and scary) but looking into that precious face and holding the warm, perfect little boy I vowed:

"Torre, I know this is a big deal. I don't know what to do to be a good mom or how to do it, but I do know what not to do. Every generation does it better than the last and knowing what not to do is the first step. I will learn to do it better. I promise to tell you every day that you are loved and it will be more than just words. You will KNOW you are loved. I will make sure you are safe and grow up to be able to stand on your own two feet and take care of yourself. I have to be sure that if I'm not here to take care of you, I need to know you can take care of yourself."

I think because I made good on my promise and showed Torre he was loved, four years later I was blessed with my next miracle: my baby girl Cortney. The doctor (who was like the father I never had) blessed me with the chance to partici-pate in her delivery.

Unsure but excited, I placed my hands around this precious little angel as her arms were freed from the womb. At the di-rection of the doctor, I gently guided her little body the rest of the way into the world. It was unbelievably empowering to be just a small piece of this miracle. She was so tiny, my fingers easily interlaced around her. I brought her to my chest, pro-tectively cradling her in my arms as the two of us met for the first time on the outside. I knew immediately she was a gift of beauty and strength beyond words.

The bond of the miracle of life is the greatest purpose God has ever given me. He made me mother and, rather than the pain and abandonment of my childhood, my true story of love began with my new life as mother of my two children. I am forever grateful. My children are now parents themselves and have made me "Grandmother" five times. I love knowing they, too, know the gift from God that lasts a lifetime.

Forever thankful this Mom remains.

Teresa Ward

CO-PARENTING WITH GOD

I am the proud mother of two wonderful boys. My journey to motherhood was a miraculous one, overcoming obstacles like endometriosis. As all mothers can attest to, sometimes our children can get into situations with the potential for dire consequences. My son, Brandon, had one such experience. If it weren't for God speaking to me in a dream, I believe things could have turned out to be devastating for my son.

Several years after my sons were born I went through an incredibly difficult time in my life. I needed something specific to penetrate the darkness that had enveloped me. I was reading through Psalms and Proverbs every single day, desperately longing for hope, encouragement, and direction, but nothing came of it. One day I remember having the television on a Christian station and I heard a man say, "God could be speaking to you in your dreams." My spirit leapt with anticipation because I dream all night every night and have since

I was a child. I wondered if it could be that God was speaking to me?

I began to write my dreams down and learned to interpret them according to scripture. Many of my dreams began to come to pass and I was utterly astounded! I was infused with hope that God was specifically speaking to me and He cared about every detail of my life. I sought out the man from the television and began studying under him and later became an instructor for him; I needed to be sure I understood what God was saying. For years following, God Himself would reveal what my dreams meant and would show me each time how they aligned with scripture.

God began to lavish me with extravagant gifts called dreams wrapped in biblical wisdom. I now had a whole new arsenal of weapons for raising my children. Weapons of mass instruction: of warnings, insight, encouragement, prayer strategies, glimpses of the enemy's plans, struggles my children were dealing with in their heart, root issues, and prophetic dreams of things to come. I cannot tell you how many times a dream revealed a choice my children were about to make so I could warn them in advance, in hopes they would make a different choice. Sometimes they heeded the warnings and sometimes they didn't, later regretting it. Many times, when they were acting out, God would use dreams to show me what was really going on in their hearts, so I could address the real issue. God would give me strategies and then cover us all with emotional healing through His loving grace.

One of the most profound dream interventions for my children was concerning my oldest son, Brandon. The dream was very brief, but the essence of the dream revealed I didn't have much time and I was to begin a Daniel fast immediately for my son. (A Daniel fast is a 21-day fast abstaining from certain foods just as Daniel did in scripture.) Upon awakening from that dream, I obeyed and began a 21-day Daniel fast, praying earnestly for Brandon.

Very late one evening, 22 days later, there was a knock at the door. It was the police. They were looking for Brandon and said he had been accused of kidnapping and rape by the parents and brother of a young girl Brandon knew. I knew my son and knew this allegation was not true. Brandon has an incredible gift of compassion and loves helping the underdog. He will stand up for someone despite what other people think. This accusation was not in line with his character at all. I told the officer I would do everything I could to help locate him. The officer gravely explained that the charges, if proven true, would mean a minimum of 10 years in prison.

I would be lying if I said I wasn't distressed. I contacted the girl's parents with the help and permission of the police, to assure them I knew my son and I felt their daughter was safe. I also assured them I would do everything I could to help. At this point, I did not have the whole story, and I felt for the parents. I knew how I would feel if I was in their situation. I immediately got on the phone to Brandon and left him a message to let him know the police were looking for him and that I wanted to know what was going on. He called me back right away.

"I don't care what they accuse me of. I am protecting her. She is being abused at home and I am not going to let them hurt her anymore! I don't care if I go to jail because this is the right thing to do."

I eventually convinced him to trust me and to trust God and to let me bring Brandon and the girl to the police station so the police could see she was okay. When we got to the police station, we stood in front of the officers who were there to arrest my son. It was a terrifying moment, and one you never expect to have as a parent. The officers took this young woman's statement. (She was seventeen years old and therefore was allowed to speak for herself.) She explained Brandon had done nothing wrong and that he was, in fact, protecting her from an abusive situation at home. Brandon was taken for questioning, but later that same day was absolved of all charges.

After taking her statement, the police urged this young woman to return home to try and work things out with her family. "Will you please drive me?" she asked me hesitantly. "I am afraid of what they will do to me."

I nodded. "I'll wait outside until you let me know you're okay."

The moment she entered her house, the screaming started. I could hear her stepfather screaming at her inside the house even though I was parked clear across the street at a local park. I wasn't sure what to do so I just waited. This beautiful young girl eventually came out of the house, almost catatonic, and in obvious trauma. She said her mother intentionally left the room and her stepfather threw her over the coffee table and began to push and hit her. She was trembling as she got back into my car, with her stepfather on the front porch screaming for her to never come back.

I immediately called the police to explain what had just happened and get advice on what to do. The police advised us to keep our distance from this traumatized young girl because of the recent accusations against Brandon by her family. Her family could still press charges.

At her request, I dropped her off at the home of one of her friends. The next day this beautiful young girl tried to commit suicide. Thankfully, God saved her life but sadly I don't know how she is doing today.

Later, as I was alone in prayer, I suddenly remembered my dream. It occurred to me that all of this took place the day after the end of my 21-day Daniel fast for Brandon. I wept with gratitude that within 24 hours, Brandon had been cleared of all charges and that the girl was still alive. I'm not sure what things would've looked like had I not been praying and fasting. I'm just grateful God loved Brandon enough to have me intercede for him so he could be protected from the plans of the enemy.

I have hundreds of similar (though not all are so intense) stories about dreams that involve my children, ranging from scary to laugh-out-loud hysterical. Co-parenting with God for me has been a dream come true... Or should I say hundreds of dreams come true?

Laura Fleetwood

I REMEMBER

I was tempted to toss the darn scooter into the street. Whose idea was this, anyway? Oh wait...it was mine. It had seemed like the perfect solution to start our days in a good way; I'd get some exercise pushing the baby in the stroller while my 4-year-old practiced on her new scooter. We'd all get to breathe in the fresh air, soak in vitamin D, and enjoy God's creation. A win all around! Let's call them "morning walks," I thought proudly. It's just what we need.

I had been staying home full-time with my girls for about a year at that point, and I'll be honest: the days were long. Really long. It was as opposite as one could imagine from the fast-paced corporate environment and daily affirmations of a job well done that I had been used to for the past decade. I wasn't finding a groove in this motherhood deal, and it stung. But this idea of daily walks in the morning sparked a new possibility within me. I envisioned my post-pregnancy tummy slimming with each stride and lovely chats with my sweet little girls. Maybe we could even bring our journals and sketch trees, bugs or other fun finds.

What I had not imagined on these magical morning walks was the skinned knee several blocks from home, the meltdown in a cul-de-sac over a smashed worm, or the temper tantrum refusal to ride the scooter one more inch at the bottom of a steep hill yet to climb. Plus, I forgot the snacks.

How did I get here?

I carefully balanced the scooter between my hands and stroller, kicking it with each step. I bribed the screaming preschooler with the promise of a snack and vowed to scratch "morning walk" from the daily to-do list. I also may have snapped at the girls and cried.

Upon our return home I prepared our promised snack: an apple cut horizontally to show the magical seed star. I was done and wanted to call it a day. I was a failure. I couldn't even take my children on a fun walk without tears.

Those early years were tough ones for me. "Failure" was the main label I plastered all over myself. I was a failure at doing fun things. I was a failure at keeping it all together. I was a failure at preparing healthy meals. I was a failure in every hope-filled endeavor I had planned for my motherhood role. If I could give that younger me a word of encouragement or advice in that moment, this is what I'd tell her:

Time has a way of softening all the fears. Be kind to yourself.

Tell someone about your frustrations. It doesn't make you a bad mom. It makes you a better one.

No mom has it all together. Not one. Not now. Not ever.

Do the best you can. God will fill in the gaps.

Cereal is just fine for breakfast, lunch or dinner.

Find the activities that bring you joy and do them. Every day. Your children are watching. It's one of the best gifts you will give them.

Fast forward to today, 8 years from the scooter drama. (Those days were long, but oh my, the years were fast.)

I am sitting with my girls, reminiscing about the past: "Hey, mom," my oldest recalls enthusiastically. "Remember when we ALWAYS took those morning walks? We ate apples and had so much fun. Let's do that again sometime."

"Yes, love," I reply smiling. "I remember. I really do."

Lisa Anne Tindal

LEAVING LOVED

I wore red that day, attempting to inspire myself. My mama wore red and she wore it well. So, I wore red last week, anxious to appear in control and assured like mama. I met with people, several that day. One, rather outspoken and sure of herself in a way that made me, twenty years her senior, feel uncertain. She avoided my eyes and kept glancing toward my neckline. At first, I thought: *This necklace is cool; I guess she wonders where I got it.* Her fixation continued, becoming a question. I figured it out. I decided: *It's my turkey neck, lines like tissue paper crumbled up then folded back to be used again.* The lines in my neck, that's what she's obsessing over.

Later, with many encounters between, I stood in my bathroom and there it was: all day long I'd worn my sweater backward, the stitching of the tag showing as a rectangle at the little hollow place at the base of my neck. Surely, someone thought to tell me but decided against, not wanting to ruin my day. I wondered why people let me carry on all day, afraid to reveal the truth. It reminded me of the time when my children finally decided to speak their truth, revelations of their heart-held angst no one else had been brave enough to confront.

When it happened I decided, something's wrong, like need-to-see-a-doctor wrong. She was out of control. There were words I'd never heard her say and they were loud, so loud; I backed away afraid of what might happen. She screamed. I cried, loud wailing pleas, "Why are you doing this? Please stop!" She told me I'd disappointed her. I'd lost her respect. She told me she needed things from me she'd never gotten and how I'd compensated in ways she'd never really wanted. For days, we did not speak. She still lived at home, only home now felt like an overnight stay in jail, no one to call. I, the convict; my crimes exposed. It nearly broke me before I saw it all for what it was: she'd finally spoken. My daughter is vocal. She is resilient and self-reliant. She is all those things now; but she wasn't when I decided she was the tough one who kept us all together. She longed not to be depended on, to not be the one without need, to not be my star.

Being the parent of adult children is laborious and good, it's redemption in my self-examination, in their courage to confront my mistakes and manipulative behaviors from a distance. It's a circling back around, learning lessons from them, their decisions and words, finally sharing hard things they'd never been bold enough to say before.

I see it now, harshly sweet. The time my daughter wore the green gator uniform, little sneakers, a big ribbon in her hair and huge pompoms. She followed the other four-year-olds toward the court, then turned and ran for the bathroom to throw up. The time she was selected for the 4-H speech competition, and we drove to another town, her grandma and I, to have her give the speech I made "just a little better here and there." Looking back now, oh, my lord, she had only just completed her speech therapy for the R's she couldn't say. But, I was proud, "Look at her, judges, see what she can do!" See what I have done. I see it now. Thank you for showing me easy, my children. In my arranging your futures, in what I thought was right, was love, I could have worn you out, led you to flee. I now see it made you strong, strong enough to let me know, courageous enough to move past it all to become who you are.

Soon, it happened again, this revealing of truths held back. This time it was my son. I was offended this time and found his declaration mouthy and arrogant. He, soft spoken, matter-of-factly said: "My life doesn't revolve around baseball like yours does."

"Well," I said, turning to face him with my hands on my hips, my pride spread out between us in the kitchen one early morning before school. "My life doesn't revolve around baseball, I'm doing this for you."

He calmly replied. "Yes, it does." And then told me he had "no intention of settling, of wasting his academic abilities at some podunk school because he just wasn't good enough to get recruited for a big one."

Still, I thought he would, because I thought he could.

Later, I'd find my note, balled up and tossed in the trash, the one that said: "I'm sorry if I made baseball bigger than you wanted it to be." My heart sort of hurts still as I imagine him reading it and shaking his head, his handsome upturned lip, cynical as he crushed the paper in his fist, maybe thinking, "Why did it take this long for you to see?"

We'd driven eight hours to show off for baseball coaches. He never said a word, only nodded when asked about food.

Eight hours with him pretending to listen to music or to sleep, I was driven. I made sure he pitched there, on the field where the Braves trained for their season. He was worthy. Coaches noticed. He was capable and strong; it just mattered very little except for how much he knew it mattered to me. We'd hurry to tournaments, chances to be seen. He'd change in the car and just sit sometimes, no words, just letting me spew motherly motivational ramblings about his talent and then he'd turn his long, lean body towards the window to open the door. I'd pop the trunk latch and he, with heavy bat bag, walked toward the dugout. If you'd told me then that any of this was wrong, I'd not have believed you. I always said, "I love you." He said, "Love you too."

I thought of being a mother last night, as I do in some way or another every day, praying they sense God near, hoping they remember my "Don't forget I love you!" notes. My son had gone back to college from Christmas break, and I'd forgotten somehow, so I thought for a second, *I wonder what he's doing?* before the emptiness reminded me of his departure. My daughter, a newlywed at home with her sweet husband. I thought of texting her but didn't. I'll wait until tomorrow. I'm still tentative with her, wanting her to continue to grow strong, resilient.

I'm almost certain that if you asked someone who knows me they'd say it was good, the way I raised them up, the way they knew my love. I'd like to know if there'd been one attentive observer who thought about telling me the truth I know now. So, if you asked that circle of friends, family or maybe a social media observer if I'd been a pushy mama, a controlling mama or a mama who sought glory through her son, her daughter, they'd maybe say, "No way" or "Not Lisa."

The truth comes gradually; a harsh reality when your children get just far enough away to tell you so, far enough from the fear of their mama's reaction. Brave enough to know the value of honest expression despite causing their mama's shoulders to drop and her eyes to turn away as they become warm with tears.

Neither of them would hurt their mama; our journey had been rocky, single mama for a bit, just us three. My daughter, my son, and my vulnerable and striving heart, they became children who pleased.

When you raise children who know they are your whole life because you've told them so, the message can get a little murky. When you strive to give what you long to have had, you can become driven and unaware your children have become a gauge of your worth, puppets for your show. I sent emails to teachers, explaining the hard years; surely my daughter should be recognized in some way. I spent lots of money and time on things they had fun with but were content without. I nominated my son for induction to a club, noteworthy and aspirational; yet, he never participated.

Today my daughter is a nurturing teacher, giving and focused on setting a tone for learning in four-year-olds. My son attends a rigid military school. He turned down a rank of honor, yet is focused on good grades. A tiny part of me wonders, one day maybe, "Teacher of the Year!" or his name listed after four years with his photo under an academic award called "Gold Stars." Recognition may come, be deserved but, unprompted by me, without my compelling and forceful manipulation.

I read about another mother, Rebekah, last week. I'm not sure how I'd missed her part in the story, the one in the first book of the Old Testament about brothers and soup bowls, goat hair-covered hands and maternal conniving. The one brother, skillful and robust, the other reclusive and unattractive. I read about the comparisons she made and her plans to make exchanges, to have one favored over the other. I'm not a scholar of biblical lineage, ancient laws, and rituals of parenting. The divine purpose of this family, perhaps in the smallest of ways, I see now is for me. I saw myself in Rebekah and thought she must have felt justified in her attempts to make Jacob something other than what God had decided he would be. He loved his mother just as intently, did as she said and so he followed her instructions; Isaac was fooled. Isaac questioned the voice, the timeliness of the hunt, the serving of the meat, but drew him near and blessed him saying, "Come near and kiss me, my son." (Genesis 27: 26 ESV). I wonder if she felt joy or shame over her cunning manipulation. I wonder if she'd become so intent on forcing her idea of best that she became blind to the desires of her sons, the bond of the brothers, the design of God.

Adulthood comes and the unraveling overwhelmed Rebekah. She saw the hatred between her sons; her control had become uncontrollable. Decisions were going to be made, wives would be taken, futures she despised would likely come to pass. It all became clear, the undoing of all she'd done. She said to her husband, Isaac, "I loathe my life." (Genesis 27:46 ESV) But, Rebekah loved Jacob. (Genesis 25:28 ESV) Rebekah loved her son. Like the last words in a well-written book, I read them again and am sure Jacob knew, from the time she cradled his tiny body, to the times he was obedient to her prideful wishes and demands, he was loved. Still, he fled and she died before he came back, before she might have had the opportunity to hear his grown-up complaint, before the situation and relationship could be redeemed.

What a solemn place God brings us to, the place of seeing your plans mislaid by your prideful misleading. A place when life shows you precisely who you've been and then leads you gently, but not without heartache, through it. It's grace that comes from our children when, despite our mistakes, they love in new, less demanding ways. Just last week, there was an unexpected telling me so, an invitation for time together. We call them "mommy days" or an unexpected confirmation of my love spoken in a grown-up way, more than "you too."

I'm so thankful they told me. I've not thought for a long time of my daughter's confrontation, my son's setting me straight. I treasure my children's hard lessons taught. I delight in them as individuals with hearts and minds healthy enough to become themselves and to go their own ways, leaving loved.

Misti Coker

WHEN I CAN'T FIX IT

Her crystal blue eyes looked at me as if she were three again. "Momma, fix it!" they said.

The doctor had just told us the news we didn't want to hear, nor did the doctor think he was going to find: Cancer. The small six-letter word that changes lives forever.

Cancer is an atrocious word for anyone's ears, but to young newlyweds it is the unthinkable.

My daughter's husband had begun having trouble swallowing. It had gone on for months. She told him to go to the doctor, but he put it off. It gradually got worse. Food wouldn't go down and he felt that liquid was just dripping. He lost 15 pounds in a week. We knew something was wrong, but we thought maybe just a procedure to stretch his esophagus would work. Through the help of others, they got an appointment with a gastroenterologist who immediately scheduled an EGD.

I didn't have to go, but as a mother I didn't want my daughter to sit alone as her husband had this procedure. After the procedure, we went in to see her husband in the recovery room. Our first question was if he could swallow better. We were expecting him to say, "Of course, I can!" but, instead, he answered, "I'm not sure."

The doctor entered the room and I knew by the look on his face it wasn't good. When he said he had found a "mass" I realized it wasn't going to be a quick and easy fix. My daughter began to ask the doctor questions and my mind shifted into "Fix-it Momma" mode. What can I do? What can I say? How can I make this better? How can I fix it?

On that sweltering hot day in July, my daughter and her husband were thrown into a storm, and they couldn't simply click their ruby red slippers three times and get back to Kansas. They were in the eye of the hurricane where the wind and water were swirling around them. They were drowning, or at least they thought they were. From one doctor's appointment to the next, the news got more terrifying. My daughter, who is a nurse, knew and understood everything the doctors were saying, and that scared her even more. So many rounds of chemo, so many treatments of radiation, and then surgery: the removal of a rib and puncturing of a lung was followed by a long hospital stay. The road was long, and the journey was going to be a tough one.

Questions began filling my daughter's brain. Was he going to survive? Were the treatments going to make him more ill? How was she going to continue working a twelve-hour afternoon to morning shift at the children's hospital? How was she going to continue her schoolwork in her nurse practitioner's program? How were they going to pay the bills? Were they going to be able to have children after all the treatments? How did this happen? What was God trying to tell me? What am I going to do? Why? What? When? How?

I yearned for the days when my daughter was little and she had small worries. I wanted to pick her up, hold her tight and say, "I will fix it." But that wasn't going to happen. I wanted her life to be pain free. I wanted her and her husband to celebrate and do what young married couples do. I wanted her to start planning for a family. But cancer had invited itself in and planned to stay awhile.

My momma job now included cancer; something I had prayed wouldn't bless us with its presence. I started asking questions again. What was my new job description going to consist of? Since I couldn't fix it, what could I do as a mother? What could I do to ease the pain? What could I do to relieve some worry?

It was time for me to suit up and go out on the field of play. Just like a football game, this cancer game was going to be filled with first downs and setbacks, along with touchdowns and fumbles. I had on my cheerleading uniform and I was gripping my pompoms.

I began every day with prayer. I would find myself not only praying first thing in the morning, but every time I thought of my daughter and her husband. "Pray without ceasing" was my new motto against this enemy. I also set a personal goal to bring joy to every day for them, whether it was through something large or something small. I began by gathering a team and getting them all to huddle up. I recruited my friends, my daughter's friends, and our family, and we became the EMT'S (Emergency Motivational Team) for my daughter and her husband. I assigned everyone a date to send in any type of little surprise. I created a motivational wall out of metal in their

kitchen where they could hang uplifting messages with mag-
nets. I cleaned. I went to the grocery store. I cooked. I made
motivational positive posters. I took them to dinner, gave
them spending change, and sent them flowers and cards, but
the most important thing I did was to become a large listening
ear.

I should be honest. Many days and nights I cry. I cry because I can't fix it. I cry because I'm sad. I cry because I'm
fearful cancer may creep back in. I'm terrified that I can't pre-
vent heartbreak and pain. I yearn for my daughter not to have
to deal with cancer. BUT I can't fix it; all I can do is be the
cheerleader and let her know, without a doubt, she can count
on me.

Tina Wright

THE UNPLANNED PATH

I did everything right, or so I thought. I graduated high school and college. I settled down into a solid career and then waited for the next steps. I knew marriage and family were just around the corner. (With at least one of my children inheriting my curly hair, of course.) As months stretched into years, I waited and watched as friends and family found their "someone's" and got married. But I didn't see a "someone" on the horizon for me at all. I would look around wishing I could scream, "I'm right here! See me?"

And then the hard part started. I watched these same friends start to have babies, and the ache in my heart grew heavier. I began to worry. Was I ever going to be a parent and hear that little voice say "Mommy, I love you,"? I began to question my worth. I thought I was a good person. If that were true, though, why wasn't God following my plan? Surely the vision I'd had since I was little about being a mom was from

Him, right? I put on a brave face, gritted my teeth when I was asked (over and over) why I wasn't married and pretended I was okay with just being the favorite aunt.

At age thirty-six (and still single) I resigned myself to the fact that God and I were obviously not in sync. I had very clearly seen a certain vision and path for my life, but when this vision failed to materialize, I began to question my faith. I even considered not listening to Him ever again if it was only going to end in hurt. So you can imagine my internal struggle when I heard Him tell me to take the first steps to becoming a foster parent. And was it a struggle!

On the one hand, this was my opportunity to mother and make a positive impact on a child by giving them a loving home – even if it might just be temporary. But I was hesitant. I was unsure of God's voice now. What if I was hearing Him wrong again? Putting my fear aside, I decided to step out and take the chance.

I became a first-time foster parent in January of 2014. That was an experience in itself. But it was my second placement that would forever change my life. In June of that same year, I welcomed a one-month-old bouncing baby girl into my home. I got to experience motherhood almost as if I had birthed her myself. I relished the middle of the night feedings and cuddles, the first coo, the first laugh, crawl, step, word, and hug. I was in love, but the foster parenting journey is a treacherous one for your heart. As a foster parent, you're supposed to want to help keep families together, but when your heart gets invested in the child you're caring for as if it's your own, it's scary to think she could be taken from you on a moment's notice. The rest of that first year I spent relishing the wonderful moments and praying through the tough valleys. It was motherhood in the truest sense of the word.

While on a family vacation in July of 2015, I received a call asking if I would be willing to take on another newborn baby girl. This time there was not a shred of indecision. I leaped at the chance to once again love on a tiny miracle.

In February of 2016, I finally became a "mother" in the legal sense of the word when I officially adopted my oldest daughter, Jayden. The adoption of my youngest, Tallie, made us a family of three. While no court of law could have told my heart before the adoption that these girls weren't mine, it was a wonderful thing to know that, now, no one could take them from me.

I can look back and remember standing at the crossroads of the choice to be a foster parent. I paused wondering if I should follow the path I was currently on of waiting for God to make me a mother in the way I wanted Him to, or choose to take a huge step onto the path where the end destination was unknown and the rewards unclear. You see, God already knew which path I would take. He knew had I stayed on the path I was on, it would have kept me stagnate and wallowing in self-pity. He had chosen my destiny the second I was created. He had hand-picked my daughters for me before they were born and woven our hearts together forever. He knew His way to unite us was going to be on a path I hadn't even considered for my life.

Today, I'm so thankful for every moment of sorrow, of anger, and for all the "Why not me?"-s. Those moments were the catalyst that pushed me down an unlikely path toward motherhood. The fear of the unknown has been replaced by the indescribable joy I feel when my daughters tell me "Mommy, I love you."

Renee Greene

MOTHERHOOD: THE FAINT OF HEART SHOULD NOT RIDE

Every good and perfect gift is from above.
James 1:17 (NIV)

I am truly blessed to be "Mom," "Mama," "Mother," or whichever name my children choose to call me. It's music to my ears. However, motherhood has not always been easy for me. It's been a roller coaster ride with terrifying hills to climb and exhilarating downhill coasting to enjoy.

My journey started at the base of a steep climb, beginning with the struggle of infertility. While navigating my way through this, I had a co-worker who had a personal relationship with Jesus (I did not). She would talk to me about His faithfulness, grace, and mercy. She planted a seed, but it just sat in my heart unfertilized, like my barren reproductive system.

After an unsuccessful year of trying to get pregnant and a myriad of doctor's appointments, I learned I have Polycystic Ovarian Syndrome. This means I don't produce "good eggs" or ovulate. The hill grew steep as we entered the twists and turns of fertility tests and treatments. But through it all I had this unexplainable peace. Peace because I believed, no matter what, I would have a child whether through fertility or adoption. I felt God promised me this although the seed of a personal relationship with Jesus still lay dormant.

I began to crest on this ride when we received the news we were pregnant with our first child after our very first attempt. After a fairly uneventful pregnancy, our son was born. We were overjoyed! This ride was actually becoming enjoyable.

Soon after, with the help of modern medicine, I conceived again. This time, with a baby girl we named Paige. We were thrilled when we heard the news! I allowed my mind to dream for months about what my little girl would look like and how different a girl would be from having a boy. I was walking on air... until the day she was born. That was the day my heart was broken, my hopes and dreams shattered. Our daughter was stillborn.

As I sat in the hospital bed holding Paige's little body in my arms and admiring her ten tiny fingers, ten tiny toes, and her enormous beauty, I was filled with a pain there are no words to explain. The only crying in the room was my husband's and mine. As my tears fell, they watered that tiny seed planted years ago in my heart by my co-worker. The seed quickly began to bloom. I supernaturally knew in that moment Jesus did not forsake me and He would be the only one to get me through the most agonizing pain I have ever felt. The foundation for my future recovery from years of depression and debilitating anxiety was laid the day Paige went to Heaven.

That was the day I encountered Jesus and allowed Him into my heart.

When I went to my doctor shortly after Paige was stillborn, he asked me if I wanted any medication to help me. I told him "No." I knew I needed to feel this pain, no matter how tremendous it was, to cross through it to the other side. I was overcome with sorrow (I cried for seven and a half weeks straight) knowing I would never mother Paige here on earth. My hopes and dreams for her life had died with her. Yet, through it all, I believed there was purpose in my pain.

Even amid my deep grief, I experienced a season of exhilaration, a downhill breakaway on the ride, so to speak. Three months after Paige was born still I became pregnant on my own with our third child. I embraced this miracle! I had been told I would never get pregnant without fertility treatments. We celebrated God's faithfulness as we experienced the safe arrival of our son four days before his sister turned one in Heaven. The ride, though still painful, was joyful again.

I knew in my heart God was healing me. What I didn't know was He was about to completely break me - my body, and mind - to completely heal me.

In the months after my second son was born, life became one long, unending trip up the steepest climb of the tallest roller coaster hill. My severe anxiety increased with every clack of the uphill climb. I constantly thought I was dying of a brain tumor or cancer. I feared my husband's death. I feared something would happen to one of my sons. These thoughts consumed me, the battles were debilitating, and they left me broken. I can clearly recall one family trip where it was particularly bad. As we were driving, I had pains in my head and feared a brain tumor was growing. I truly believed I was dying and I remember telling myself, "This is it. I'm not coming back from this trip. I'm going to die." Yet the peace of the Lord surrounded me. I knew Jesus was with me and because of that was able to continue on.

My brokenness also manifested itself in the form of PTSD, depression, an increase in my eating disorder, and severely unhealthy control issues. It led to the brokenness of my family, my husband, and my children. My marriage was falling apart. My kids were emotionally hurt.

Going to a chiropractor healed the pain in my head (I learned I had a rib out of place) and at least I no longer feared I was dying. This reprieve didn't last long though. Within a few weeks I was riddled with anxiety again and it manifested itself in insomnia. I was a mess. Every day the question of "How am I going to sleep tonight?" consumed me because I never did. I just lay awake and grew more and more anxious.

After a month, I finally told my husband I felt I needed to go to the emergency room. As I sat with a nurse and told her what was going on, she told me she felt I was transferring my anxiety and grief from the death of Paige to other things in my life: my health or my husband's or sons' lives. I left the hospital with prescriptions and a referral for a therapist.

Soon after this visit to the ER, I had an amazing friend speak God's truth to me. She lovingly explained I was trying to hold on to Paige and keep her alive when the truth was she was in Heaven with Jesus. By holding on to her so tightly, I was neglecting my family and causing a stressful environment in my home.

I knew it was time to say goodbye to Paige and let the Lord take care of her, while I took care of the family in my home. My greatest fear had been that letting her go would mean forgetting her and not acknowledging her as part of our family. I now can trust God that will never happen. Paige is with God and He has given me two wonderful, creative, funny, sweet boys to mother here on earth. I decided to release Paige to God because I knew I would see her again in eternity.

I wish it had ended there, but it didn't. Two months later, I decided I didn't need medication anymore and stopped taking it cold turkey. That was on a Thursday. For the next three days I was bedridden with anxiety and depression. Finally, the following Monday I had a breakthrough. God had been telling me for some time He wanted me "to come out of the darkness and into the light." I knew He wanted me to be free from the shame of two incidents of sexual abuse in my past, but I hadn't been ready, until that Monday. I immediately got out of bed and told my husband. Admitting my deep-rooted pain was my low point. Completely broken, I had finally hit the place where God could begin rebuilding me. I went to my therapist that day and shared with her that I didn't feel like living anymore. We both agreed to my immediate hospitalization

Looking back, I now realize when I said I didn't feel like living anymore, it wasn't that I didn't want to be alive, I just didn't want to live the way I was living anymore – riddled with anxiety and depression. I wanted to be free of it. That decision to admit I didn't want to live like that opened the door for Jesus to fully capture my heart, and in my complete faith and trust in Him my healing began.

At the next appointment with my therapist following my hospitalization, he asked me, "Through all of this, did you still believe in and trust God?"

My answer was simple, "Yes, it is He who got me through."

During my hospitalization, new tracks of restoration and healing were laid. In the weeks and months afterward, as I continued to be rebuilt, my marriage also experienced healing, and our boys began to recover. God also began healing me of my 20-year battle with an eating disorder: I left the hospital at 88 pounds but in three months' time, I had gained 20. By God's grace, I was finally emotionally and physically healthy.

With each passing season of motherhood, I realize how valuable the hills, loop-de-loops, and even derailments can be. I wouldn't change even one of the hills of this motherhood roller coaster ride. I would choose again to get on and endure the pain and embrace the joys because that choice has made me who I am today: an emotionally, spiritually, and physically healthy woman who is present for her husband and children and always carrying her daughter in her heart.

Motherhood, like roller coaster rides, is not for the faint of heart, but with each twist and turn I have grown stronger, more compassionate, more joyful, and more faithful - all because I choose to ride.

Jennifer Frickie

PROVERBS OF MOTHERHOOD

Motherhood is a slow process of refinement. The physical, mental and spiritual trials a mother faces, from the moment of conception until her last breath, are truly overwhelming. No matter how many children a woman has, she is always learning to be a mother because each child and stage of life is vastly different from the others. Every day challenges a mother in their patience, wisdom, gentleness, kindness and self-control. Motherhood is the steel blade of God that refines and sharpens a woman's faith and character.

The weight of responsibility a mother carries is enough to bring her to her knees. Her tears pour out easily with joy or sorrow, relief or fear. A mother's tears are tiny prayers that cannot be contained. They spring forth at a moment's notice, corroding her young supple skin into pathways of wrinkles. She ages with each tumble, head bump, and bruise. Silver hairs sparkle in the sunlight, marking the late-night fevers, bad dreams and tummy bugs.

A mother is a new creation with each passing day as all self-ishness is slowly stripped away. With red, swollen eyes and a dry throat she will struggle to pull herself up, stumble to the kitchen to pour milk into sippy-cups and make breakfast with a smile. She will watch her kids eat their breakfast and coax them to take a few more bites before the busy day begins. Later, as she serves lunch she'll realize she forgot to feed herself and her long-forgotten coffee will now be an iced latté.

At bedtime, a mother faces the challenge of bending a strong will without breaking it - or herself - in the process. She sees herself in the defiant looks and sneaky endeavors. At first, she is slightly amused and proud of her child's strength and determination; nevertheless, she quickly determines that defiance must be defeated. She knows if her child will not submit to her authority, they may never submit to God's. She will cry on the hallway floor as her toddler kicks the door.

Motherhood teaches a child to appreciate her own mom in ways she never did before. She will recall her own rebellion with regret as she now understands the anguish she caused her mother. She will call home and say, "I am so sorry, Momma."

A mother will hope her child never makes the same mistakes she did, but knows sometimes it's the only way a child will learn. So, a mother will stand by waiting for her baby to run into her arms so she can soothe the pain of a lesson learned the hard way. A mother loves unconditionally and forgives all things, ever willing to forget an offence.

A mother might forget the first time her baby says "Mama" or "I love you" but she will always remember how it made her feel. She will not remember much of the early years because sleeplessness and post-partum depression cloud her memory. But she will stare at pictures and videos on her phone each night, hoping she will not forget.

A mother's heart will break in a billion different unexpected ways. She will feel it shatter when she looks at the ultrasound screen and sees the lifeless body of her baby in her womb. She will weep on her knees when she miscarries a second time. Undaunted, she will conceive again and hope to hold her baby in her arms. And yet, on a cold, rainy day she will watch her children go crazy in the house and question her life choices.

A mother's feelings are contradictions. As her child's independence increases, she rejoices and yet her heart aches because she is losing her baby. One morning she looks at her little one and notices their pajama pants are two inches too short. Her chest tightens in pain as she realizes that overnight her baby became a toddler whose cheeks are no longer chubby. In the excitement for the baby to grow up, she forgot to enjoy the last tender moments of late night feedings and early morning cuddles. A mother will look back and long for those sweet baby hugs and sticky kisses.

A mother is still learning to be an adult as she prepares her children for the real world. Shielding them from the darker troubles of this world while she grapples with the sins of humanity. She will pray optimistically for her children's future as the shadows of war and chaos cover the Earth.

Motherhood will turn a woman into a warrior fighting for the survival of her babies no matter the cost. A mother steps into the trenches of war between humanity's sinful nature and the call of sacrificial love. There will be sacrifices both great and small. She will begin sacrificing as she watches her body transform in pregnancy. Her body is charted with stretch marks, yet a mother will rejoice at the large bump that forces her to waddle through a store as strangers stare and giggle. But that is only the beginning. As she defines her maternal role she will find that some friendships become casualties of motherhood. Job opportunities will be passed because the baby comes first. Too many cocktails will be missed as she waits for the baby to no longer need her milk.

A mother will struggle to be who she was before. She will slowly adjust her standards and expectations of how things should be. She will struggle to balance her desire for cleanliness and daily accomplishment with the reality of toddler messes and tantrums. Her mini-van will always have crumbs and toys. She will regularly struggle to run errands while dragging two toddlers and a baby from store to store.

A mother will be in bed by eight o'clock. At late night events, she will daydream of her pajamas and cozy bed. Socializing will bring her anxiety because she doesn't know how to talk to adults anymore. Words like "yuckies" or "ouchies" slip out far too often.

Motherhood is isolating. The friendships she once had will fall into the periphery. She will learn to be intentional about planning playdates. Yet, at least a third of the playdates will be canceled for various reasons. She will cling to her phone as a source of connection with the outside world. Texting is her ally because telephone conversations are cursed with screaming and madness erupting within the home.

A mother's home will be her sanctuary, and yet at times feel like a prison. The endless loads of laundry feel soul-crushing, while some days she will carelessly push it off the couch and read books and snuggle the little ones. Some days a mother will feel successful: the kitchen's clean, laundry folded and dinner ready on time. Other days a mother will sulk in feelings of failure as the house is littered with toys and mountains of dirty dishes threaten to crash down like an avalanche.

Motherhood challenges marriage. A mother can't shave her legs as often as before and she does not feel romantic wearing pajamas with spit-up on the shoulder. She will try to straighten up the house and put on her best smile when her husband walks through the door at night, but her messy bun with a large pink bow, leftover from playing dress-up, will limp to the side and give away the fact that she is tired and only desires to escape to dreamland. She will look at her husband hoping he will offer to let her shower and go to sleep, only to see his weary eyes beg for the same thing.

A mother will read books about how to raise children and have a happy marriage at the same time because a mother constantly wonders if she is doing a good job. She will worry about ruining her children. Are they spoiled? Are they learning enough? Will they be strong enough to succeed in the real world? She will silently scold herself for losing her temper and being harsh.

A mother is often overwhelmed by all the roles she's been cast in. She's the cook, accountant, maid and teacher. She's the photographer, event planner, chauffeur, stylist and nurse. She's everything to her babies and husband, always wondering if she's enough. She will look in the mirror at the new wrinkles and silver sprinkles in her hair. She will not see herself anymore. She is someone new. She is a mother. Her eyes are full of resilience and wisdom as she laughs at her momentary vanity, knowing more wrinkles and silver sprinkles will come.

The future is uncertain for everyone, but no one is more aware than a mother. Each day brings new battles.

A mother is a peacemaker brokering truces and setting boundaries.

A mother speaks life and hope into the hearts of her children. She is the fountain from which her children drink. She tenderly directs their hearts to love, while firmly stamping out bad behavior.

In her later years, a mother will enjoy the fruits of her labored sacrifices and realize that through the various challenges she was strengthened and made wise.

A mother is like a diamond. As the woman is forged under the holy fire of motherhood, she becomes a miraculous creation that God ordained to shine as an imperfect reflection of Him.

MEET THE AUTHORS

Aubrey Atkinson

Aubrey Atkinson is a mid(ish) 30's gal, born and raised in Atlanta, but has affectionately called Charleston home for the last ten years. She spent a good many years traveling the states and abroad after college while all her friends were settling down and starting families. Once she settled in Charleston, she met her husband of five years through a series of random circumstances. (However, don't be surprised if he tells you it was through MySpace!) You can most often find her working out (or at least dressed like she did), drinking lukewarm coffee, or at a local brewery- (with her hubs and twirls in tow!) She chronicles her escapades at For the Love of Mom Genes on Instagram and Facebook and is revamping her blog so stay tuned.

Connect with Aubrey:
Facebook: For The Love of Mom Genes
Instagram: @fortheloveofmomgenes

Lara Busold

Lara Busold is a magazine editor and freelance writer from Northeast Ohio. She loves being home with her husband Bryan, and her three amazing kids, James, Grace, and Caroline, and their dog, MJ. She is thankful to know Jesus, and tries every day to be more and more like Him.

Connect with Lara:
Facebook: Lara Busold

Misti Coker

Misti Coker began her professional career as a teacher after earning a Bachelor of Science in Education and Master of Science in Education, specializing in reading. During her teaching career, she taught at various levels and then became the Literacy Director for her school district. It was because of her work in education and knowledge of how to raise test scores that she began presenting workshops for high school teachers entitled "Teaching Secondary is Elementary." After twenty-three years of teaching and training she decided to learn in other areas and received certifications in Life Coaching with emphasis in Hope Coaching, Grief Coaching, Marriage Coaching, Stress Management Coaching, Soul Care, Suicide PAIR, Adolescent Sexuality, and God Identity.

Misti is the author of a children's book, *A Little Bit of Hope*, wherein all proceeds are donated to the Brooklyn Project. She also started the Blessed Hope Project for cancer patients through FUMC Stuttgart's Pass on Joy committee. Painting for a local business is one of her favorite hobbies, and she donates fifty percent of the proceeds from her products to Blessed Hope.

Connect with Misti:
Facebook: Pass on to Press On
PassOnToPressOn.com

Laura Fleetwood

Laura Fleetwood encourages women who are tired of trying to keep it all together. Through vulnerable, authentic storytelling, Laura reminds you there is always HOPE, and you are never alone. You can find Laura's story about burnout and breakdown along with words for Messy Miracles at seekingthestill.com.

Connect with Laura:
Facebook: Seeking the Still
Instagram: @seekingthestill
SeekingTheStill.com

Jennifer Frickie

Jennifer Frickie graduated from Virginia Tech with an English degree in Creative Writing and a minor in Leadership. She is married to her college sweetheart, Justin, who is an Officer in the Marine Corps. She is the mother of Rebecca (4), Diana (3) and Joshua (8 months). Combining her passions for the Bible and writing, Jenny aims to empower others to attain the freedom Jesus Christ paid for on the cross.

Connect with Jennifer:
Facebook: @TempleDetox28
Instagram: @jdfrickie.templedetox28

Renee Greene

Renee Greene is a child of God, a wife, and a mother. She is the author of the book *In the Stillness: Making Room for God to Move* and a blogger at www.singanewsongministry.com. She lives with her husband, Mark, their two boys, and their dog, Cocoa Puff, in Mount Pleasant, South Carolina. She enjoys reading the Bible, being still in her quiet time with Jesus, and listening to praise and worship music. She also enjoys walking, running, reading, writing, gardening, and the beach.

Connect with Renee:
Facebook: In the Stillness
Instagram: @inthestillness08
singanewsongministry.com

Stephanie Haynes

Stephanie Haynes is a Co-Founder of Relevant Pages Press where she serves as a Writing Coach for first-time authors. She educates writers on the back-page responsibilities of authorpreneurship on the RPP blog, and helps authors build an engaging speaking platform to share their stories with a listening audience.

Stephanie is also the owner of Stephanie Haynes Consulting (StephanieHaynes.net) where she teaches women to build balanced lifestyles and love their lives. She regularly shares her schedule management strategies on her Calm the Chaos blog and as a speaker at women's events across the country.

As an author, Stephanie has self-published three books designed to bring the reader into a deeper peace so that they might experience joy in both the chaotic and calm seasons of life. Her passion is to revolutionize the way women live their lives, helping them to fulfill the promise of Jesus that He came so we can have an abundant life.

Stephanie graduated from CSU Chico, is a graduate of She Speaks (Writing and Speaking tracks) and a graduate of Jenni Catron's Cultivate Her leadership coaching program. She and her husband have two kids and two rescue dogs and live in St. Louis, Missouri.

Connect with Stephanie:
Facebook: @stephaniehaynesnet
Instagram: @StephHaynes_SHC
Twitter: @StephHaynes
StephanieHaynes.net

Allison Mayfield Herrin

Allison has always been a survivor! Sexual abuse, abandonment, divorce, heartache and more! All of which led to stupid choices during adolescence. As such, she has been a single mom most of her children's lives. She is a self-proclaimed, mistake-makin mess learning to live with a heart of reckless abandon to a God knows all of her mistakes but continues to be her gentle and loving teacher through all of them. Her passion is women...strong, fierce, brave, warrior women! Her greatest desire is to help women discover their inside voice that encourages them to be who they were born to be and to stop listening to the outside voices that tell them who they ought to be.

She is not a professional counselor, pastor or anything of the like; just a southern girl saved by grace desperately trying to live a life worthy of being called a follower of Jesus!

She is the Founder of MAIA Moms, an organization dedicated to single moms and their children and you can also find her blogging over at allisonherrin.com

Connect with Allison:
Facebook: Allison Mayfield Herrin
Instagram: @allisonherrin
Twitter: @allisonherrin
AllisonHerrin.com

Betts Keating

Betts Keating is the author of the book *My Movie Memoir Screenplay Novel*, a memoir occasionally interrupted by a screenplay. She currently resides in South Carolina with her husband and two daughters. In a former life, she worked full-time as a graphic designer in various ad agencies and publishing companies in NYC. In this life, she is learning how to balance her work as a freelance graphic designer and an author, with her starring role in the long running series called Motherhood. She is an avid connoisseur of all things TV and movie and often enjoys comparing herself to fictional characters.

Connect with Betts:
Facebook: Betts Keating Author
Twitter: @bettskeating
bettskeating.com

Angie Kutzer

"Inspiring Good Choices, Perseverance, and Forgiveness" is the tagline for Angie Kutzer's ministry. Angie started "From My Life to Your Heart," out of her passion to share her life and her faith. Angie is a Public Speaker and has been blogging for 2 ½ years at her Blog "Gifts from God – Perspectives of a Busy Mom." From My Life to Your Heart also creates and daily shares encouraging and uplifting social media images about life and faith, with the intention of helping bring happiness and positive support to others. These images are available on Instagram, Twitter, and Facebook.

Angie is currently working on her first book, and looks forward to a future of serving others by inspiring and encouraging them in whatever way she can. If you need a Speaker for an upcoming event, please consider Angie; she strives to equip her listeners to: *Walk seamlessly through life's challenges with inspiration and honesty. *Learn to fully forgive so you can have a life of joy & serenity. *Win over daily stress with a new perspective of peace. *Be empowered to move forward, making good choices for your future. *Embrace real life by turning trials into triumphs and hectic days into humor.

Connect with Angie:
Facebook: @frommylifetoyourheart
Twitter: @frommylifetoyou
Instagram: @frommylifetoyourheart
frommylifetoyourheart.com

Tiffany Pate

Tiffany Pate lives in Tega Cay, S.C., is a coffee lover and a spastic blogger. She juggles three kids and coffee cups with her amazing husband, Chris. When she's not chugging coffee and kissing boo-boos she's teaching others about essential oils or leading ladies in Holy Yoga at Draw Near, a women's creative worship retreat. Tiffany might wear many different hats, but two of her favorites are loving on others and speaking life into moms around the country.

Connect with Tiffany:
Facebook: MrsTMPate
Instagram: @mrstiffanypate

Kimberly Ritter

For more than two decades, Kimberly Ritter has been selling homes in the Carolinas as a full-time Realtor, annually recognized as a "Top Seller" in the Charleston area. She holds a B.S. from the University of North Carolina at Greensboro, and is a member of the South Carolina Association of Realtors (SCAR) and the Charleston Trident Association of Realtors (CTAR), and National Association of Realtors (NAR).

Kimberly is blessed to be a wife, mother, and grandmother. Alongside her husband, Tom, Kimberly leads in the marriage ministry called "Re-Engage" at their church and strives to use her experiences in marriage to help other couples strengthen and renew their marriages. She has recently begun a blog called CornerstoneChat.com where she plans to share about her life and the lessons God has taught her.

Kimberly and Tom enjoy traveling, sunset cruises on the Intracoastal Waterway, and live in Mount Pleasant, South Carolina with their dogs, Trigger and Remington.

Connect with Kimberly:
Facebook: Kimberly Self Ritter
CornerstoneChat.com

Robin Stearns Lee

Robin Stearns Lee has been in love with words ever since her grade school writing assignment in which she described her younger sister as a child "who could cry for hours but never shed a tear." She is a wife, mother and grandmother, and a retired administrative assistant for BP Chemical Company. Robin earned an Associate in Arts with emphasis on English and Writing from Trident Technical College and attended the College of Charleston, both in Charleston, South Carolina. Her writings have appeared in local newspapers, online in Lowcountry Literary Life, and she has a short children's story titled "The Girl Who Hated to Read" available on Amazon.

Robin writes a blog which chronicles her travels as a retiree as well as her husband's cancer journey. She leads a local book club and enjoys writing book reviews on her Facebook page. Robin is originally from Pine Hills, Florida, but now makes her home in Jamestown, South Carolina.

Connect with Robin:
Facebook: Robin Stearns Lee
RobinStearnsLee.wordpress.com

Lisa Anne Tindal

Lisa Anne Tindal is married, the mother of two, and the Executive Director of a small non-profit. Prayer, writing, walking and painting are her prescriptions for the often-heavy days her work may bring.

For as long as she can remember, she's written letters and notes to herself. A note in the back of her journal says, "If I wrote a letter to everyone I know about how God has changed my life, brought me through and made me whole...that would be my book." Discovering this note was the beginning of her blog, "Quiet Confidence" and a new Bible for Christmas inspired the title of the book inside her soul. She is in the beginning stages of this memoir called, *The Colors of my Bible.*

Connect with Lisa:
Facebook: Lisa Hendrix Tindal
Twitter: @itwaslibby
Instagram: @lisanne811
lisanne3015.wordpress.com

Harriet Turk

Harriet Turk knows that life can be challenging and joyful. She relates to the hopeless journey to be a superwoman that so many of us travel. As a parent and a professional, Harriet believes it's time for us to stop pretending our lives are perfect. Her life is messed up, and she believes your's is, too. Yet, for some reason, we keep thinking that everyone else has it all together, so we pretend that we do as well. Harriet believes it's too much work and too hard to be fake. This is why as a motivational speaker, she delivers her "get real" message of resilience and being true to yourself. For her, it's not just a talk, but a way of life. She inspires others to embark on an exciting adventure of self-discovery.

Harriet lives with her teenage son, Andrew, in Memphis, Tennessee, and believes Memphis barbecue is the best on the planet. Don't try to say otherwise, she won't listen.

Connect with Harriet:
Facebook: Harriet Turk Fan
Instagram: @harrietturk
harrietturk.com

Sandy Tyson

I am a mother of two children who have families of their own, making me a "gramma" of five. Both "Mother" and "Gramma" have been names I have been blessed to be called and qualify me with a "Mom Phd.;" my finest privilege in life. I live in Saint Louis, Missouri and have always desired to be a writer. This honored selection has been an inspiration to put pen to paper in my future.

Connect with Sandy:
Facebook: Sandy.Tyson.94

Teresa Ward

Teresa Ward is a disciple of Jesus Christ. She is the founder of the ministry Above & Beyond and the author of *Gateway to Dreams - 3 Simple Steps to Dream Interpretation*, published by Destiny Image Publishers. Teresa travels around the world teaching people how God speaks in dreams, visions, and a multitude of other symbolic ways. She is the proud mother of two grown sons and currently lives in the Charleston, South Carolina area.

Connect with Teresa:
GatewaytoDreams.com

Vicky Willenberg

Vicky Willenberg is a wife, mother, and obsessive volunteer at her sons' school. She works as a Senior Digital Marketing Manager and freelance copy editor. Vicky also chronicles the good, the bad, and the hysterical on her blog The Pursuit of Normal. You will most often find her on Facebook, sharing the daily shenanigans that go hand in hand with raising two boys while still growing up herself. Her work can be found in *Scary Mommy's Guide to Surviving the Holidays*, The HerStories Project anthologies: *Women Explore the Joy, Pain, and Power of Female Friendships, My Other Ex*, and *So Glad They Told Me*. She has also been published on to following blog/websites: Scary Mommy, TheMid, BlogHer, Mamapedia, and Mamalode.

Connect with Vicky:
Facebook: The Pursuit of Normal
Instagram: @thepursuitofnormal
thepursuitofnormal.com

Tina Wright

Tina Wright is an avid reader who fancies herself as a wanna-be part-time writer. After graduating college with a Bachelor's degree in nursing she left her small town in Pennsylvania to work as a travel nurse throughout the United States before finally settling down in 2006. After living the high life as a single woman, she began the tedious process of becoming a foster parent. God's plan came to fruition in 2016 when she finalized the adoption of her first daughter and then again in 2017 when they became an official family of three. Life is crazy busy for these girls but it wouldn't be half as fun if it wasn't. Tina and her sassy sidekicks reside in Hanahan, SC.

Connect with Tina:
Facebook: Tina R Wright

Publishing your book is possible!

Relevant Pages Press was created by authors for authors. From the beginning of the writing process through publication and beyond, we seek to educate and serve writers who want to pursue their dream of self-publishing their books.

We offer:

Pre-Writing Services: For the writer who wants guidance and accountability.

Project Management Services: For the writer who is ready to take their completed manuscript through the process of publication.

Social Media Management Services: For the writer who wants to build a platform and become a successful "authorpreneur."

Message Development Services: For the writer who wants to build sales through book signings, book talks, and other live events.

Make your dream come true today!

RELEVANTPAGESPRESSLLC.COM

www.ingramcontent.com/pod-product-compliance
Lightning Source LLC
Chambersburg PA
CBHW021928170626
46807CB00007B/3022